Bread Baking for Beginners

+

Healthy Smoothies Cookbook

2 IN 1

An Easy Guide with 100+ Recipes to Make at Home

Andrew Flores, Ted Davis

All rights reserved.

Disclaimer

Sommario

Bread Baking for Beginners

An Easy Guide with 50+ Bread Recipes to Make at Home

Andrew Flores

All rights reserved.

Disclaimer

INTRODUCTION

Bread is a traditional, well-known foodstuff that existed in our latitudes long before potatoes, rice or pasta. Since bread not only provides energy, but also vitamins, minerals and trace elements, the product is predestined as the basis of a diet.

Bread as a diet basis Bread as a diet basis

The bread diet was developed in 1976 at the University of Giessen. Since then, a number of modifications have been made, but they only differ from one another in nuances. The basis of the bread diet is the high-carbohydrate food bread.

Bread is made from grain, so bread can differ depending on the type and processing of the grain. Products with a high whole grain content are preferred in the bread diet. Such breads are characterized by a high content of trace elements and minerals, they also contain fiber. Heavily processed white bread is not prohibited in the bread diet, but should only be consumed in small quantities.

HOW DOES THE BREAD DIET WORK

The bread diet is basically a diet that works by reducing the intake of calories. The total amount of energy for the day is reduced to

10

1200 to 1400 calories in the bread diet. With the exception of a small warm meal made from grain products, these calories are only supplied in the form of bread.

This does not need to be dry meat, low-fat quark with herbs or strips of vegetables. There are hardly any limits to the imagination, which explains the large number of recipes for the bread diet. The drinks included in the bread diet include water and tea without sugar. In addition, a bread drink is taken before each meal to aid digestion and stimulate the immune system.

BENEFITS OF THE BREAD DIET

Unless self-deception is committed when placing the sandwiches, one advantage of the bread diet, as with most low-calorie diets, is quick success. But the bread diet has other real advantages over other diets. The diet can be designed to be very balanced so that no deficiency symptoms are to be expected.

In principle, a bread diet can therefore even be carried out over a long period of time without any adverse health effects being expected. Another advantage is the ease with which the diet can be carried out. Most of the meal is cold and can be prepared. As a result, even a working person can easily carry out the diet by eating the bread they have brought with them instead of eating in the canteen.

DISADVANTAGES OF THE BREAD DIET

The bread diet does not have any particular disadvantages resulting from its composition. However, if the bread diet is only carried out temporarily and then returned to the previous lifestyle, the dreaded yo-yo effect also occurs with the bread diet. During the hunger phase during the diet, the body's basal metabolic rate decreased.

After the end of the diet, weight gain therefore occurs rapidly and usually to a higher level than before the start of the diet.

GLUTEN-FREE BREAD

Servings:1

INGREDIENTS

- 250 g   Flour, dark, gluten-free
- 150 g   Flour, light, gluten-free
- 100 g   Buckwheat flour
- 1 cube Yeast, fresh
- 1 ½ tsp   salt
- 430 ml Water, warm
- 1 ½ tbsp Chia seeds
- 2 Tea spoons\ Apple Cider Vinegar

PREPARATION

Dissolve the fresh yeast in the warm water.

Mix 500 g gluten-free flour - I often use the mixture as stated above - with the salt, vinegar, chia seeds and the yeast-water mixture with a wooden spoon, so that no more flour is visible.

Cover the bowl well and let it stand in the refrigerator for at least 12 hours up to 5 days, possibly longer.

You can bake whenever you feel like it and have the time. Take the dough out of the refrigerator at least 2 - 3 hours before baking, do not stir again so that the structure is not destroyed. Pour into an oiled rectangular cake tin and cover and leave in a warm place.

Do not preheat the oven. Bake at 200 ° C top and bottom heat for about 60 minutes. Remove from the mold and bake for another 10-15 minutes. Apply a knock test.

Tip: This is a flexible recipe, possible variations with bread spices, grains, seeds, carrots and herbs.

INGREDIENTS

- 500 g Flour
- 5 tbsp oil
- 3 tbsp Cocoa powder
- ¼ liter milk
- 350 g sugar
- 1 teaspoon cinnamon
- 2 Tea spoons baking powder
- 400 g Hazelnuts, whole

PREPARATION

Mix the dry ingredients, add the oil to the milk and mix with the
dry ingredients to form a smooth dough (which can be a little
tough). Spread on a greased baking sheet and spread the hazelnuts

15

on top and press into the batter. Bake for about 40 minutes at 160 - 170 degrees, it can turn lightly brown!

Remove from the tray and immediately cut into the desired size, e.g. biscuit size.

Tip: If you like it, only spread about 2/3 of a baking sheet, then the whole thing will be a little thicker.

MARES AFTER 3 MINUTES - BREAD RECIPE

Servings:1

INGREDIENTS

- 450 ml milk
- 500 g   Flour (wheat flour)
- 1 cube yeast
- 2 tbsp sugar
- 2 prizes   salt
- 2 tbsp vinegar
- 100 g   Raisins
- 100 g   Chocolate, in pieces

PREPARATION

Mix the yeast with the warm milk. Add all other ingredients and process well. Put in a greased dish and put in the cold oven. Cut lengthways after 10 minutes. After 40 minutes, brush with milk or whisked egg yolk.

Servings:4

INGREDIENTS

- 90 g Whole wheat flour
- 60 g Wheat flour type 550
- 150 g water
- 1 ½ g Fresh yeast
- 60 g Rye flour type 997
- 60 g water
- 1 g salt
- 12 g Yeast
- 60 g Wheat flour type 550
- 50 g water
- 6 g Yeast
- 240 g Wheat flour type 550
- 150 g water

19

- 90 g Spelled flour type 630
- 12 g salt
- 12 g olive oil
- 50 g water

PREPARATION

Pre-dough

For the pre-dough, mix together all the ingredients (90 g whole wheat flour, 60 g wheat flour (type 550), 150 g water (20 degrees Celsius) and 1.5 g fresh yeast). Then let ripen for two hours at room temperature and another 22-24 hours at 5 degrees Celsius. Rye

Sourdough

For the rye sourdough, mix together all the ingredients (60 g rye flour (type 997), 60 g water (45 degrees Celsius), 1 g salt and 12 g starter items) and let ripen for 12-16 hours at room temperature.

Wheat sourdough

For the wheat sourdough, mix all the ingredients (60 g wheat flour (type 550), 50 g water (45 degrees Celsius) and 6 g pitchers) together and let ripen for 6-8 hours at 26-28 degrees Celsius. Then store for 6-12 hours at 5 degrees Celsius.

Autolysis dough

For the autolysis dough, mix 240 g of wheat flour (type 550) and 150 g of water (65 degrees Celsius) and let rest for 60 minutes (dough temperature approx. 35 degrees Celsius).

Main

dough For the main dough, the pre-dough, rye sourdough, wheat sourdough, autolysis dough together with 90 g spelled flour (type 630), 12 g salt, 12 g olive oil and 50 g water (100 degrees Celsius) for 5 minutes on the lowest setting and a further 5 minutes second stage knead until the dough temperature is around 26 degrees

Celsius. Do not pour in the hot water slowly until you have mixed the other ingredients a little.

Let the dough mature for 60 minutes at room temperature. After 30 minutes, stretch and fold.

Gently round the dough and put it in a proofing basket floured with rice or potato flour with the end facing down. Cover with foil and let ripen for 8-10 hours at 5 degrees Celsius.

Bake bread

With just a little cooking and the end up at 250 degrees Celsius, falling to 230 degrees Celsius (after 10 minutes switch down), bake in the pan for 50 minutes.

INGREDIENTS

- 500 g Flour
- 350 ml water
- 1 cube yeast
- 1 ½ tsp   salt

PREPARATION

Put everything in the bread maker or make a yeast dough in the normal way - leave to rest for approx. 90 minutes. Then form rolls and then simply bake in a preheated oven at 220 degrees for about 20-25 minutes.

Sprinkle with sesame seeds or poppy seeds to taste before baking.

For approx. 9 - 12 rolls, depending on the desired size.

POTATO CAKE - CAN ALSO BE BAKED GLUTEN-FREE

Servings:1

INGREDIENTS

- 300 g Potato (s), cooked, pressed through the press
- 1 cube yeast
- 1 teaspoon salt
- 300 ml Water, lukewarm
- 1 pinch (s) sugar
- 500 g Wheat flour, whole grain or
- Flour, gluten-free
- 1 teaspoon marjoram
- 150 g Ham, diced
- 6 tbsp Pumpkin seeds, possibly more
- n. B. Bread spice mix

- Water for brushing
- Possibly. Egg yolks for brushing

PREPARATION

Dissolve the yeast and sugar in the water, let rise for 10 minutes. Mix the flour with salt and marjoram. Add the pressed potatoes and the yeast, knead thoroughly and let rise well (the volume should roughly double).

Roughly chop 4 tablespoons of the pumpkin seeds and knead into the dough together with the ham cubes. Shape a dough ball and put it in a mold (I like to use Tupper's Ultra). Brush the surface with water or a mixture of water and egg yolk, sprinkle with the remaining seeds (press lightly). I also like to use a few more seeds for the dough.

Let rise again for 15 minutes. Bake at 200 ° C (fan oven 180 ° C) for about 60 minutes.

If you want to bake the bread gluten-free: You don't need more liquid than specified, otherwise the dough will be too heavy and the bread will be sticky.

BREAD ROLLS LIKE FROM THE BAKERY

INGREDIENTS

- 333 g   Flour type 405
- 125 ml water
- 100 ml milk
- 7 g Dry yeast
- 1 tbsp sugar
- 1 teaspoon, heaped salt

PREPARATION

Mix all ingredients well and let the dough rise at room temperature for about 1 hour. Shape the dough into rolls and place on a prepared baking sheet.

Let the rolls get a light tan in a hot oven at 190 ° C for about 15 minutes, add a key of water if necessary. Then briefly set the oven to about 200 ° C and bake the rolls for about 5 minutes until they have reached the desired brown color.

MANNIS MIXED WHEAT BREAD

Servings:6

INGREDIENTS

- 400 g   Rye flour, type 1150, alternatively 997
- 600 g   Wheat flour, type 550
- 680 ml Water, about 38 degrees warm
- 42 g Yeast, fresh
- 75 g   sourdough
- 17 g Iodized salt
- 15 g sugar
- 50 g margarine

PREPARATION

Knead all ingredients into a dough with the kneading machine.

The kneading time should be at least 4-6 minutes so that the dough is nice and smooth and develops good adhesive properties.

Make sure that the dough does not get too soft if you do not want to bake the dough in a mold. Let the dough rise for about 15 minutes and then shape it into a roll.

Place the rolling pin on a baking sheet with parchment paper and sprinkle it with water. First heat the oven to 50 degrees and let the dough ferment in the oven for about 20-30 minutes.

Spray with water every now and then.

When the rolling pin has reached the desired volume, remove it from the oven. Heat the oven to 250 degrees and turn the temperature down to 210 degrees and put the tray with the bread in the oven. Now pour 1/4 cup of cold water on the bottom of the oven and close the oven door. Open the door briefly after approx. 3 minutes so that the steam can be drawn off.

Personally, I work the dough into a ball and place it in a floured proving basket. When the volume of the dough has reached the top, I place a baking sheet on the proofing basket and turn the whole thing so that the dough is now on the baking sheet. Leave the basket a little longer so that the dough loosens and the basket can be removed without sticking.

Total baking time approx. 50 minutes with convection. Varies depending on the type of furnace.

If necessary, turn the temperature down to 200 degrees.

MULTIGRAIN SEED BREAD

Servings:1

INGREDIENTS

- 400 g Sourdough, whole grain rye
- 200 g   Spelled flour (whole grain)
- 90 g Buckwheat flour (whole grain)
- 30 g Millet, whole
- 30 g Quinoa, whole
- 30 g Flakes, (5-grain flakes)
- 30 g Pumpkin seeds
- 30 g Sunflower seeds
- 30 g linseed
- 30 g sesame
- 12 g sea-salt
- 10 g Turnip tops
- 200 g Water, warm (approx.)

- 10 g Yeast, fresh, optional (*)
- 3 tbsp Seeds - mix of sesame, sunflower seeds, flax seeds, pumpkin seeds and 5-grain flakes)

PREPARATION

Knead all ingredients except for the seeds to be sprinkled into a homogeneous dough (food processor, approx. 7-10 min).

Cover and let the dough rest in a warm place for 30 minutes and then knead again briefly (2-3 minutes).

Sprinkle the shape of the BBA or a box shape with half of the seeds for sprinkling. Pour in the dough and smooth it out. Then sprinkle with the remaining seeds. Let the bread rise again in a warm place (1-3 hours, depending on the leavening power of the sourdough and the addition of yeast).

Baking:

BBA : Bake the bread with the "Bake only" program for 1 hour.

Oven: Bake the bread at about 200 ° C for about 50-60 minutes. (Since I always bake bread in the BBA, the information for baking in the oven is only a guide.)

Then let the bread cool down on a wire rack and leave it to rest in the bread box for a day before cutting.

The specified amounts are sufficient for a bread weighing around 1000g.

THREE KINDS OF PARTY BREAD

Servings:10

INGREDIENTS

- 1 package   Baking mix, for farmer's bread
- Something salt
- 650 ml Water, (lukewarm)
- For the filling:
- 75 g   Ham, raw, diced
- 3 tbsp Cheese, heaped, Grana Padano (very young Padano and finely grated)
- 1 tbsp. Oregano, dried
- 4 Tomato (s), dried, pickled in oil
- 1 tbsp. Oil, (from the dried and pickled tomatoes)
- 3 tbsp Sunflower seeds
- 3 tbsp Poppy
- 3 tbsp Sesame, (unpeeled)

- 75 g   Salami, air-dried (cut into small cubes)
- 6 Olives, black (core and then cut into pieces)

PREPARATION

Knead the dough according to the instructions on the packet, but let rise for at least 2 hours.

In the meantime, grate the cheese, chop up the salami, ham and tomato.

Divide the dough into 3 equal parts. Knead a chunk of dough with cheese, tomato pieces and oregano and shape into an elongated loaf.

Knead one part with the ham cubes and shape into an elongated loaf and knead the third part with the salami pieces and olives, also shape into an elongated loaf.

Turn the ham and salami bread in the grains and let rise for another 30 minutes.

Preheat the oven to 250 degrees (top and bottom heat), place the bread on a wire rack (lined with baking paper) and put it in the hot oven.

Place an ovenproof dish with water in the oven and pour half a cup of water directly onto the hot oven floor, close the door immediately. Bake the bread for 10 minutes at 250 degrees, turn the heat down to 180 degrees and bake for another 25-30 minutes.

Glaze the hot bread with a little hot water, glaze the cheese and tomato bread with the oil.

Alternatively, 12-15 mini party rolls can be made from each lump of dough. Then reduce the baking time to 5 minutes at 250 degrees and 8-10 minutes on reduced heat.

You can of course play with the encores as you like. This is how it becomes the "rum-fort-bread"

Of course, this is even cheaper and better with self-mixed flours, but especially for bread-baking beginners or rarely bread bakers, the mixture is simply the best way not to lose interest and most so-called bakeries only use mixtures (a shame). I cannot recommend bread makers. The breads are far from being as beautiful as they are in the oven, they have holes and are not in an attractive shape.

1 HOUR BREAD

Servings:2

INGREDIENTS

- ½ liter Water, lukewarm
- 1 cube yeast
- 400 g   Spelled flour
- 100 g   Buckwheat flour
- 1 teaspoon   salt
- 2 tbsp Fruit vinegar
- ¾ cup Sunflower seeds
- ¾ cup sesame
- ¾ cup linseed

PREPARATION

Knead all the ingredients. Bake for 1 hour at 220 degrees. When baking, put a refractory bowl of water in the oven.

The dough doesn't have to rise. If necessary, let the bread cool overnight.

LOAF

Servings:1

INGREDIENTS

- 500 g   Flour, (bread flour)
- 300 g water
- 10 g salt
- 1 bag   Dry yeast, or 20 g fresh yeast
- 1 pinch (s) Bread spice mix, optional

PREPARATION

Preheat thinner stones in the oven for 1/2 hour at 190 ° C top and bottom heat, thick stones for 1 hour so that the stone is hot enough and the dough does not stick. If you are not entirely sure, it is better to preheat the stone a little longer.

Knead all of the ingredients by hand or in a food processor to form a smooth dough that should be relatively firm. Cover and let the dough rise in a warm place for about 1 hour. Just before the bread goes into the oven, put a bowl of water in the oven or fill the drip pan with water and slide it under the stone. This creates the so-called steam that makes the bread crispy. Shape the dough into an elongated loaf. Brush the top of the bread with water with a brush or by hand. This creates a nice crust. Then put the bread in the oven or place it on the stone.

During the first half hour the bread should only be baked with lower heat, in the second half hour only with upper heat. Much higher temperatures are stated in many recipe books. We have had good experiences with 190 ° C.

Tips:

With white flour (cake flour) you can also use 2 tablespoons of (herbal) olive oil and only approx. 250 ml of water.

You can also prepare the dough the evening before. The dough is then placed in a cool place, e.g. B. in the refrigerator, stored for about 12 h. The next day the oven has to be preheated and the dough comes straight into the preheated oven. He does NOT have to go again in a warm place. This method makes the dough particularly fine-pored.

Bread flour can now be bought under this name in many (organic) shops. It only contains wheat and rye flour, no dry yeast or salt (pay attention to the list of ingredients!).

LOW CARB BREAD

Servings: 1

INGREDIENTS

- 300 g low-fat quark
- 8 m.-large Egg (s)
- 100 g Almond (s), or hazelnuts, ground
- 100 g Flaxseed, crushed
- 5 tbsp Wheat bran
- 2 tbsp Flour, or soy flour
- 1 pck. baking powder
- 1 teaspoon salt
- 2 tbsp Sunflower seeds
- Butter, for the mold

PREPARATION

Preheat the convection oven to 150 ° C and hold the heat for 15 minutes before the dough comes into the oven.

Mix the quark, eggs and baking powder in a bowl with a hand mixer (whisk), then add the other ingredients and stir well again. Pour into the greased dish (25-30 cm) and sprinkle with the sunflower seeds. Bake at 150 ° C for at least 90 minutes.

The dough is quite runny and the finished bread is very moist / moist. That can be changed with more bran.

The finished bread should be stored in the refrigerator in a bag that is not tightly closed. It also freezes well.

Advice from Chefkoch.de: Since the cadmium content in flaxseed is relatively high, the Federal Center for Nutrition recommends not consuming more than 20 g flaxseed per day. The daily bread consumption should be divided accordingly.

MUESLI ROLLS OR MUESLI BREAD LIKE FROM THE BAKERY

- 300 g   Wheat flour, (whole grain)
- 200 g   Wheat flour (type 550)
- 10 g   salt
- 10 g   Yeast, fresh
- 20 g   honey
- 350 g   water
- 200 g   Dried fruits
- 80 g   oatmeal
- 50 g   nuts
- Flour for the work surface
- Something Water for brushing

PREPARATION

Roughly cut the dried fruits into small pieces. All fruits are suitable, I especially like apricots, plums, raisins and apples. Chop the nuts, hazelnuts, cashews, almonds, pecans, walnuts are my favorites.

Make a smooth dough with the remaining ingredients. Knead for at least 5 minutes. Just before the end of the kneading time, add the fruits and nuts. The dough is quite thin and sticky at first, but when it is kneaded enough it becomes nice and elastic. Cover the dough and let it rise warm for 1 hour or in the refrigerator for 6 hours.

Place the dough on a lightly floured work surface and divide into 2 parts for large loaves, 4 parts for small breads, 12 parts for rolls and leave to rest for 5 minutes. Now shape long loaves or rolls. Wet with a little water and roll in the oat flakes. Let the bread rise for 1 hour, the rolls for 3/4 hour.

Preheat the oven to 250 ° C. Cut breads as desired. Put in the oven, reduce the temperature to 220 ° C, and steam well. Large loaves of bread take 25 minutes, small ones 15 minutes, and bread rolls 10 - 12 minutes.

You don't really need a spread for this, they are sweet and hearty with a bite. Of course, jam, honey or butter still taste great with it.

Variations: You can of course make a pure raisin bread or apricot bread out of it. The types of flour can also be varied. If you don't like whole grains, try the 1050 or just 550. Instead of oatmeal, poppy seeds or sunflower seeds also taste good.

I love this bread because it is great for a sweet but not sugary start to the day and is incredibly versatile.

IMPROVED BREAD ROLL OR BAGUETTE RECIPE

Servings:1

INGREDIENTS

- 500 g Flour, type 550
- 325 g Water, 33 ° C warm
- 21 g Yeast, fresh
- 12 g salt
- 15 g Baking malt

PREPARATION

the flour in a kneading bowl and make a well in the middle. Pour the yeast, salt and 5 tablespoons of warm water into the well and stir carefully with a teaspoon. Cover the kneading bowl in the oven for about 20 minutes.

Now add the rest of the water and the baking malt and knead for at least 5 minutes to form a medium-firm dough. The dough should be between 26 and 27 ° C. Cover the kneading bowl in the oven again and let the dough rise for 30 minutes.

After the rest period, place the dough on a floured worktop, knead it briefly and fold it up so that the carbon dioxide can escape.

Preheat the oven to 210 ° C and, if possible, use a water bath, e.g. B. in the drip tray.

Because roll out or beat the dough on the floured worktop to a size of approx. 35 x 63 cm. Flour this sheet of dough thinly and divide it into large pieces of dough. (E.g. 7 x 7 cm. Then there are 10-15 rolls). It is best to cut it up with a pizza roller, spatula or knife. Place the rolls on a baking sheet and cover with a cloth.

When the oven has heated up, cut the rolls 2-3 times and spray them with water. Place the bread roll in the oven with the steam bath and spray again with the spray bottle.

Let it run for 2 minutes with top / bottom heat, then switch to circulating air. Baking time approx. 20 minutes.

SOURDOUGH WHEAT BEER BREAD

INGREDIENTS

- 300 g Whole wheat flour
- 200 g Wheat flour type 1050
- 75 g Sourdough, homemade, from the bakery or from the pack)
- 150 g water
- 150 g Wheat beer
- 1 tbsp. salt
- 1 tbsp. sugar
- 1 tbsp Bread spice mix
- 1 tbsp Baking malt
- ½ cube   yeast

PREPARATION

Make the first pre-dough the day before, mix 150 g of the whole meal flour with 150 g of water and the sourdough, cover and leave to stand overnight (8 h). The next morning, knead the rest of the whole meal flour with it.

For the second pre-dough, mix the remaining ingredients together until there are no more lumps.

Let the two dough's rest together in a bowl.

After about 2 - 3 hours, knead both dough's together for about 10 minutes. If the dough can be pulled apart into a thin membrane without tearing, you are done with kneading.

Let the dough rest again until it has risen to double its volume.

Then place the dough on a non-floured or lightly floured work surface, knead out the air and shape it into a ball, then place this in a floured proofing basket. Preheat the

oven to 250 ° C top / bottom heat, heating 2 baking trays at the same time.

When the bread has risen for about an hour and has grown significantly larger, turn it out onto one of the hot baking trays and cut into a cross at the top.

After zeroing in the oven, pour hot water onto the lower hot sheet and immediately close the oven. Caution - risk of scalding!

In 10 minute intervals, reduce the temperature of the oven in 20 ° steps to 190 ° C and bake for about 50 minutes.

Finally, place the bread on a rack for two hours to cool.

BREAD ROLLS, PERFECT LIKE FROM THE BAKERY

Servings:1

INGREDIENTS

- 500 g Flour
- 300 ml Water, lukewarm (approx. 45 °)
- 12 g salt
- 42 g yeast

PREPARATION

Knead all ingredients to a smooth dough and cover and let rise for approx. 60 minutes.

Knead again by hand and form 10 rolls of approx. 80 g each and grind round. Place on a baking sheet lined with baking paper and cover with a damp cloth. Let rise for about 20 minutes and then cut into them.

Preheat the oven to 230 ° C fan oven. Since the rolls need steam to bake, place a cup of water in an ovenproof container at the bottom of the oven.

Bake the rolls for about 12-15 minutes. They open again and become nice and plump. When they are the right color, take them out and place them on a grid covered with a cloth to cool.

SIMIT

Servings:1

ingredients

- 500 g   Wheat flour type 405
- ½ cube   Fresh yeast
- 150 ml Water, lukewarm
- 100 ml Milk, lukewarm
- 100 ml Sunflower oil
- 2 tbsp   sugar
- 1 teaspoon   salt
- 3 tbsp   Grape syrup (pekmez), alternatively sugar beet syrup
- 100 ml water
- 150 g   sesame

PREPARATION

First, stir together oil, water, milk, sugar, salt and yeast until the yeast, salt and sugar have dissolved. Then gradually add flour until the day is soft but not sticky.

Then heat the oven to 50 ° C, then switch it off again, cover the dough and let it rise for 30 minutes.

Form a snake out of the dough and divide into 10 pieces of approx. 90 g each. Then let rise again for about 15 minutes. Don't forget to cover.

In the meantime, brown the sesame seeds in a pan without fat and set aside. Warning, it pops like popcorn, but that's okay. Mix the syrup with the water in a deep plate.

Preheat the oven to 190 ° C top / bottom heat.

Shape the dough pieces into very thin snakes and tie them together. Press the ends of the cord together and first bathe the simit in the syrup and then roll it in the sesame seeds. Bake in the oven for about 20 minutes and then wrap in a tea towel to cool so that they do not become hard.

They taste good with both sweet and savory toppings and can also be frozen well.

BEETROOT BREAD FROM MY TEST KITCHEN

Servings:1

INGREDIENTS

- 350 g Beetroot
- 400 g Spelled flour type 1050, possibly a little more
- 250 g   Wheat flour, ground yourself from whole grains
- 1 bag / n Dry yeast, organic, 9 g
- 1 tbsp Sugar, extra fine
- 1 teaspoon salt
- 5 tbsp Sunflower seeds
- 150 ml sweet cream

PREPARATION

Peel and wash the beetroot, cut into small pieces and cook for about 15 minutes without adding salt. Then puree without the juice and let cool down a little.

In the meantime, weigh the flour in a bowl, grind the wheat and add to the bowl and add the dry yeast, sugar, salt and sunflower seeds. Mix the dry ingredients well. Let the cream get lukewarm and add to the flour mixture. Now stir the pureed beetroot into the dough or let it stir, I'll do that with the food processor. If the dough is not firm enough, simply add a little flour until the dough separates from the bowl.

Cover the dough and let rise for about 60 - 80 minutes. Knead again briefly and put in a prepared mold. I took a ceramic pan here and lined it with baking paper. Cut into the top of the bread and let rise for another 30 minutes.

Preheat the oven to 200 degrees. I put a bowl of cold water in the oven at the bottom.

Bake the bread at 170 - 180 degrees for about 1 hour. Check the bread with the knock test and if it sounds hollow, turn it over and let it cool down completely.

Note: the taste of the beetroot disappears completely.

RUSSIAN BREAD - VANILLA YOGURT - TART

Servings:1

INGREDIENTS

- 300 g   Biscuit (Russian bread)
- 150 g   Butter, soft
- 500 g   Yogurt (vanilla)
- 400 ml cream
- 150 ml milk
- 50 g   sugar
- 1 pck. vanilla sugar
- 8 sheets   Gelatin, white
- 10 g   Cocoa powder

PREPARATION

Roughly grate or finely chop Russian bread, mix with the soft butter and knead. Cover a cake platter with baking paper, place the 26 cm cake ring on the inside with oil, pour in 2/3 of the mixture, press it on and let it set. Put the rest on one side.

Soak gelatin in water. Whip the cream. Heat the milk, sugar and vanilla sugar in a saucepan. Dissolve the well-squeezed gelatine in it, take it off the stove and let it cool down. Just before setting, stir in the vanilla yoghurt vigorously and fold in the whipped cream.

Divide the mass, stir in the cocoa powder into part of the cream.

Spread alternately light and dark cream with a tablespoon on the base and smooth on the surface. Sprinkle the cake with the remaining crumbs and leave to cool in the refrigerator, preferably overnight. Then remove the cake ring and the baking paper. Chill the cake until ready to eat.

INGREDIENTS

For the sourdough:

- 150 g   Whole wheat flour, coarse
- 50 g   Rye flour
- 30 g   Honey, more liquid
- 300 ml Kombucha, more active

For the dough:

- 430 g   Wheat flour type 550
- 220 ml Water, warm
- 9 g Sea salt, fine or normal salt

PREPARATION

Mix the ingredients for the sourdough well the night before, then cover with a cloth and leave to rest in a warm place until the next day.

On bread baking day, mix the kombucha sourdough with all the bread ingredients in a large bowl. Then cover the bowl and let rise in a warm place.

After an hour, pull and fold the dough - do not knead! To do this, first fold one side in half, then fold the opposite side over the first half, then fold the other two sides over the first sides. Repeat this three more times - once every hour.

Then shape a bread out of the dough and let it rise for another 2 - 4 hours in a warm place.

Preheat the oven to the highest setting (240 °C, top / bottom heat) one hour before baking. Bake the bread for 15 minutes, then turn the oven down to 190 °C and bake the bread for another 30-35 minutes, or until it sounds hollow when you knock.

CUP OF BREAD

Servings:4

INGREDIENTS

- 2 cup / n Spelled flour, 812
- 1 cup   Rye flour, 1150
- 1 ½ cup / n water
- 1 ½ tsp   salt
- 8 g Yeast, fresh OR:
- 1 tsp, leveled Dry yeast
- 2 tbsp Sunflower seeds
- 2 tbsp linseed
- 2 tbsp oatmeal
- 75 ml   water

PREPARATION

Put the flour and salt in a larger bowl, dissolve the yeast with the "cold" water and mix with the flour with a wooden spoon until there are no more pockets of flour. I then put the dough in a cool room, in the hallway, basement or refrigerator for 20 hours. I usually do this the evening before, then I also take 2 tablespoons of sunflower seeds, 2 tablespoons of linseed and 2 tablespoons of oat flakes and pour about 75 ml of hot water over them, put the lid on and after the walking time add to the dough and mix in briefly.

I then fold the dough with a spatula, I do the whole thing twice. Let the dough rest for 30 minutes after each fold.

Preheat the oven to 260 ° C with a cast iron saucepan with a lid, then put the dough in the saucepan and sprinkle with grains and press firmly, put the lid on and in the oven for 35 minutes, then lower the lid, turn the temperature down to 190 ° C and Bake for another 20 minutes.

I always use very large cups with a capacity of around 300 ml.

You can use flour as you like, depending on your taste. The grains can also be omitted

ROLLS, ORIGINAL LIKE FROM THE BAKERY

Servings:1

INGREDIENTS

- 315 g Wheat flour (type 550 or 405)
- 35 g Wheat flour (type 1050)
- 15 g Baking malt
- 10 g salt
- 185 ml water
- 20 g yeast
- Possibly. sesame
- Possibly. Poppy

PREPARATION

How long have I tried and tried to finally be able to bake fresh and real rolls at home. Ultimately, I found countless recipes that look like this, but do not even suggest a relationship to a real bread roll.

In the end, two bakers helped: one with the recipe, the other with baking malt, which is very difficult to get in stores (except on the Internet).

The dough recipe is very simple and can be made very easily using the bread maker. It is best to put the ingredients in the bread maker in the following order in the evening before going to bed (dough function):

First the water, then the yeast (can also be dry yeast - doesn't make any difference), then the 550 or 405 (here too: 405 is absolutely sufficient if you don't have a 550 at hand), then the 1050. Then the baking malt and salt follow.

Without BBA, the whole thing is processed into a homogeneous dough - until it separates from the bowl. Then the dough needs about 1 - 1 1/2 hours to rest. It is best to cover it in a warm place (yeast dough).

Then you can put the dough on a non-floured work surface (I always do it on the ceramic hob) and portion pieces of 80 g each. The balls of dough must now be rounded and, if necessary, grinded or shaped into small rolls in order to loop them into "Kaiser rolls" (a good alternative to the bread roll press).

Briefly hold the dough completely under the tap and place on baking paper. You can now cut into them another 5 mm deep, if you want, and sprinkle them with sesame seeds or poppy seeds.

Then the dough pieces have to rise covered for another 60 minutes. After this time, steam the preheated oven (220 ° C top / bottom heat) vigorously and water the rolls again directly with the flower sprayer. Then put them in the middle of the oven and stay there for 18 minutes. Then take it out - let cool on a rack and enjoy.

EASTER BREAD ACCORDING TO A TRADITIONAL RECIPE

INGREDIENTS

- 1 kg wheat flour
- 2 pck. Dry yeast
- 50 g sugar
- 170 g Butter, soft, room temperature
- 6 Egg (s)
- ¼ liter Milk, lukewarm
- 350 g Sultanas, soaked
- Water for soaking
- 5 g Cinnamon powder
- 1 pinch (s)   nutmeg
- Egg (s) for brushing
- Flour for the work surface
- Possibly. Hail sugar or almond slivers

PREPARATION

Put the flour, sugar, eggs, butter, sultanas and spices in a bowl. Briefly stir the dry yeast into the lukewarm milk with a spoon, add the milk to the remaining ingredients and stir vigorously with a hand mixer (dough hook) until the dough loosens from the edge of the bowl.

Place the dough on a floured work surface and knead it extensively and vigorously. Then place in a preheated bowl, cover with a damp cloth and let rise in a warm place until it has doubled in volume (usually I let it rise for an hour, but less is also possible).

Then knead again vigorously, form two loaves and place on a tray each. Cover with a damp cloth and let rise for another 1/2 hour.

Preheat the oven to 175 ° C (convection). After proofing, brush the loaves with beaten egg and cut crosswise, then place in the oven. If you like, you can sprinkle with sugar or almond slivers beforehand. Bake the bread for 60 minutes.

You could also put both loaves on a tray, but they open quite a bit and then often "grow" together in the middle! If you don't mind, you can save yourself a lot of time. I usually cut the ingredients in half and only make one Easter bread. This is usually enough for a family of four.

PADERBORN COUNTRY BREAD, LIGHT VERSION FROM KETEX

INGREDIENTS

- 150 g Rye flour, 1150
- 150 g water
- 30 g Yeast
- 135 g Rye flour, 1150
- 150 g Wheat flour (whole grain)
- 160 g Wheat flour, 1050
- 355 g water
- 12 g salt
- 10 g Yeast, (who likes)

PREPARATION

Make a sourdough from the first 3 ingredients:

150 g rye flour 1150, 150 g water, 30 g ASG = Anstellgut.

Mix everything together and let it mature for 16 hours at room temperature.

Take off 30 g of it and give it back to the item to be placed.

Knead all ingredients and the prepared sourdough together for 7 minutes. Then rest for 20 minutes.

Then put it in a 1 kg loaf pan and let it cook.

With yeast for about 60 minutes. Without yeast approx. 120 minutes.

Bake for 15 minutes at 240 ° until the desired browning is achieved, then, falling to 180 °, bake for 45 minutes.

The bread has TA 180 and is a mixed bread 50/50.

WRONG BREAD

Servings:1

INGREDIENTS

- 160 g butter
- 2 Egg (s)
- 280 g Chocolate, grated
- 240 g Almond (s), ground
- 250 g Flour
- 4 egg yolk
- 10 tbsp powdered sugar
- Pistachios, to decorate

PREPARATION

Put butter, eggs and chocolate in a mixing bowl and beat until frothy. Then fold the almonds and flour into the dough alternately and in small portions.

Shape the dough into a roll and chill for about 30 minutes. Then cut the rolling pin into about 1cm wide slices, place them on a baking sheet lined with baking paper and bake in the oven at 180 ° C for about 10 minutes.

Mix the egg yolks with the powdered sugar, then add the chopped pistachios. Spread the mixture on the wrong breads and let it dry in the oven.

NAAN BREAD

Servings:

INGREDIENTS

- 1 teaspoon sugar
- 20 g   Yeast, fresh
- 150 ml Water, warm
- 200 g Flour
- 1 tbsp Ghee
- 1 teaspoon salt
- 50 g Butter, melted
- 1 teaspoon Black cumin
- Flour for the work surface
- Grease for the slide

PREPARATION

Put the sugar and yeast in a small bowl and mix with the warm water. Let this mixture rise for about 10 minutes until bubbles form.

Put the flour in a large bowl and make a well in the center, add the ghee and salt and pour in the yeast. Mix with a wooden spoon to form a smooth batter. Knead the dough on a floured work surface for about 6 minutes. Put the bread dough back into the bowl and cover it again for 1 1/2 hours.

Knead the dough again for 2 minutes and then divide into 6 - 8 equal portions. Shape each portion into a ball and flatten into a 1 cm thick, round, flat cake with a diameter of about 12 cm.

Preheat the grill on the highest setting. Place the bread rolls on greased aluminum foil and bake for 7-10 minutes each time - turning twice. Brush with butter and sprinkle with black cumin. Serve warm immediately or keep warm wrapped in aluminum foil.

GINGER BREAD CHENÄRAN

Servings:1

INGREDIENTS

- 300 g   Buckwheat, whole +
- 100 g   Amaranth, whole +
- 200 g   Corn kernels, (not popcorn) +
- 100 g   Brown rice, (medium grain) +
- 2 Tea spoons   Caraway seeds, whole +
- 2 Tea spoons   Coriander, grind whole
- 1 ½ tsp   salt
- ½ tsp   Cane sugar
- 2 bag / n   Baking powder (tartar baking powder)
- 3 tbsp   Sunflower seeds
- 3 tbsp   Sesame, unpeeled
- 3 tbsp   Flaxseed, whole
- 40 g   Ginger, peeled

- 250 ml kefir
- Sparkling mineral water
- Sunflower seeds, OR
- sesame
- 1 cup / n water

PREPARATION

Grind buckwheat to coriander together. Mix all dry ingredients to +. Fill up carbonated mineral water + kefir to 700 g, possibly more, add it, it has to be like a batter, rather a little more liquid, then the dough rises better. How much liquid is needed depends largely on the age of the grain. I noticed that freshly ground corn absorbs a lot. (That's why I don't use corn as breading)

Pour into a 30 cm rectangular cake pan lined with baking paper (also coated in baking pans). Place the sunflower seeds or sesame seeds on top of the dough, press down lightly. Bake in a cold oven with a cup of water at 160 ° C for 70 minutes. Needle sample.

Baking for longer doesn't do anything except toughen the crust.

Preheat with top + bottom heat to approx. 180 ° -190 ° C + bake for approx. 45-60 minutes. Leave the oven to cool on a wire rack, then remove the baking paper; if the baking paper is removed beforehand, the crust will usually be hard.

Bread pops open at the top, even if I notch the bread, gluten-free is not that easy, because the dough is very runny. But it doesn't matter in terms of taste.

BREAD CHIPS

Servings:1

INGREDIENTS

- 200 g   Bread (s) - leftovers, stale
- 125 g   Herb butter
- 75 g   butter
- 2 Tea spoons   Spice mixture, (butter bread salt, recipe from the database)

PREPARATION

Cut the bread into thin slices.

Melt the butter and herb butter and add the bread and butter salt (the recipe can be found here: http://www.chefkoch.de/rezepte/1706241279393160/Butterbrots alz.html).

Put the bread slices in the butter and wait until they are soaked.

Spread on a baking sheet lined with baking paper and bake at 180 ° for approx. 12-15 minutes with hot air until it has a nice brown color.

Let cool down and enjoy.

ULM BREAD

Servings:1

INGREDIENTS

- 250 g   Honey (synthetic honey)
- 250 g   margarine
- 100 g   sweet cream
- 180 g   sugar
- 2 Egg (s)
- 1 teaspoon rum
- 1 pck.   ginger bread spice
- 1 tbsp, heaped cocoa
- 50 g   Lemon peel
- 50 g   Orange peel
- 100 g   Nuts, mixed
- 440 g   Flour
- 1 point baking powder

Also:

- Icing sugar for the icing
- Water for the frosting

PREPARATION

Beat the margarine and sugar until frothy. If necessary, heat the artificial honey a little and then add the remaining ingredients.

Spread the dough on a greased baking sheet and bake in the preheated oven at 160 degrees Celsius for about 25 minutes.

Let the sheet of dough cool down a bit and then decorate with a frosting. Cut into small pieces of approx. 5 x 5 cm

A QUICK AND EASY RECIPE FOR BAGUETTES

Servings:1

INGREDIENTS

- 500 g   wheat flour
- 2 dice   yeast
- 300 g   water
- 30 g   olive oil
- 1 teaspoon salt
- 1 pinch (s) sugar

PREPARATION

Shape the dough into a roll on a floured surface. Then divide into 3 equal pieces and shape them into baguettes and place in the hollows of a baguette tray.

Put the tray in the COLD oven and bake the bread at 200 degrees top / bottom heat for about 35 minutes. The dough rises in the oven.

CROISSANT - RECIPE

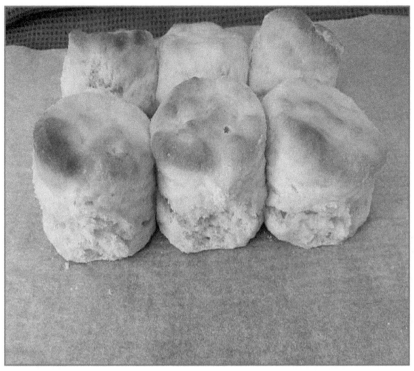

Servings:1

INGREDIENTS

- 250 g butter
- 50 g sugar
- 500 g Flour
- 1 pinch (s) salt
- 42 g yeast
- 2 Egg (s)
- 0.2 liters Milk (approximately, depending on the flour)

PREPARATION

The evening before, make a yeast dough from the ingredients listed above: Let the milk become lukewarm, mix the yeast with a little sugar and milk, leave to stand for a moment, then mix with all the ingredients except the butter. Cover and leave the dough to stand in the refrigerator overnight.

Take the dough out of the refrigerator and roll it out into a square on a work surface. Shape the butter between two cling films to half the size of the square, then dust with flour and place on the yeast dough. The flour is important because the butter must not mix with the dough, otherwise puff pastry cannot be made. So it's better to have a little too much than too little flour between butter and yeast dough!

Place the dough over the butter like an envelope, so that a triangle lies over the butter on each side and covers it. This is now rolled out into a rectangle, this rectangle is folded over each other three times and then rolled out again. You should repeat this 2 to 3 times. Then triangles are cut (about 12) and these are shaped into croissants from the broad side.

Preheat the oven to 220 to 250 ° C, this is where tastes differ: up to 220 ° C, the croissants (about 6 per tray) are baked for about 20 minutes, at 250 ° C for about 12 minutes. It's a lovely breakfast!

The recipe comes from a friend, I hope you enjoy it.

SCONES

Servings:1

INGREDIENTS

- 430 g   Flour
- 2 tbsp   baking powder
- TL salt
- 150 ml cream
- 150 ml Mascarpone
- 300 ml water

PREPARATION

Mix the flour with baking powder and salt. Sieve at least three times on a worktop and press a recess in the middle. Mix the cream and mascarpone and add to the flour with the water. Mix all ingredients with a knife just long enough that the dough just sticks together, then work on the floured work surface with your hands.

To do this, fold the dough over and over again, but only press it together with your fingertips, not with the entire palm of your hand.

Press the dough about 3.5 cm thick, just with your fingertips. Flour a round cookie cutter or a glass with a diameter of about 6 cm and cut out circles. Place the circles side by side on a parchment-lined baking sheet so that they touch. Fold the remaining dough a few times and cut out circles until the dough is used up.

Brush the scones with milk and bake in the preheated oven on the middle rack at 210 ° C for 15 minutes. Prick a stick into a medium-sized roll, if the dough still sticks to it when you pull it out, bake a little longer.

Place a kitchen towel on a grid, place the scones on top and cover with the other half of the towel.

The scones taste best when they are still warm and with strawberry jam and cream.

MIXED RYE BREAD

Servings:1

INGREDIENTS

- 450 g   Rye flour (e.g. type 997)
- 300 g   Wheat flour (e.g. type 550 or 812)
- 23 g   Sourdough (whole grain rye sourdough)
- 10 g   Lecithin (pure sunflower lecithin)
- 7 ½ g   Wheat gluten granules (contains ~ 0.3g ascorbic acid)
- 1 pck. Dry yeast (7 g)
- 17 g   Salt (iodized salt is ideal)
- 1 tsp, leveled   Caraway powder, optional
- 3 tbsp, heaped Sunflower seeds, peeled, optional
- 540 ml Water (10 ml more when using sunflower seeds)

PREPARATION

Mix all ingredients together except the water. Add the lukewarm water and knead everything for about 4 minutes with the hand mixer. Let the dough rest for 30 minutes, covered with a cloth.

When using a bread maker, put the dough in the baking machine and set a program with a total baking time of around 2½ hours.

If you want to bake in the oven, knead the dough again briefly and form one or two loaves of bread. Let rise in peace, at room temperature about 50 minutes, at 28 ° C 35 minutes are sufficient.

Bake in the oven at 250 ° C for about 10 minutes, then finish baking at 190 ° C for another 55 minutes.

BOHEMIAN DALKEN MADE FROM MOM'S RECIPE

Servings:4

INGREDIENTS

- 500 g   Flour, type 550
- Egg (s)
- 50 g   butter
- ½ cube   yeast
- 200 ml Milk, possibly a little more
- ½ tsp   salt
- Flour, for processing
- Butter, melted, for brushing

PREPARATION

Dissolve the yeast in a little lukewarm milk with a pinch of sugar. Put the flour in a bowl, make a well and add the yeast, dust with a little flour and let rise for about 15 minutes.

Heat the rest of the milk, melt the butter in it, and add the egg and ½ teaspoon salt to the flour. Knead everything together vigorously to form a smooth dough. Let the dough rise for approx. 45 minutes.

Dust your hands with flour and shape cup-sized patties out of the dough. Place on a baking sheet lined with baking paper - leave plenty of space in between, as they will still rise a little.

Let rise for another 20-30 minutes, brush with melted butter and bake in the oven preheated to 180 ° C for about 20 minutes.

Take out and brush again with melted butter.

Dalken are a must in our family with beef with dill sauce. As children we loved them with butter and honey or jam.

BREAD ROLL RECIPE

Servings:25

INGREDIENTS

- 600 ml water
- 1 kg wheat flour
- 1 cube yeast
- 2 tbsp olive oil
- 2 tbsp salt
- 1 teaspoon sugar

PREPARATION

Crumble the yeast cubes and dissolve in the lukewarm water with the sugar, olive oil and salt in the mixing bowl of the kitchen appliance, if available.

Add the flour and knead everything for a good 10 minutes with the food processor until a dough is formed that loosens smoothly from the edge of the bowl, add water or flour if necessary.

For the look and the taste, grains (e.g. millet, blue poppy seeds, sesame seeds, pumpkin seeds, sunflower seeds, flax seeds or raisins) can be added to the rolls (soak them in water beforehand for a better hold).

You can also put cheese on top or bake bacon as well as cubed salami / ham or raisins, depending on your taste.

Shape small balls into rolls, press flat onto the baking sheet lined with baking paper. Score the surface diagonally with a sharp knife and let rise under a towel for 10-15 minutes.

Then bake in the oven at 200-180 ° C for approx. 15-20 minutes until brown.

Tips:

Leave it lighter for later baking.

Put water on a second baking sheet (unless your oven can handle bursts of steam), this will make the bun crust crispier.

CORN BREAD

Servings:1

INGREDIENTS

- 375 ml water
- 1 ½ tsp   salt
- 1 teaspoon   sugar
- 1 tbsp olive oil
- 300 g Flour (type 405)
- 300 g Corn flour, fine
- 1 bag Dry yeast

PREPARATION

Mix the two types of flour well together, but do not pour into the container yet. Pour all ingredients into the container in the order given - the wet ingredients first and then the dry ones. On top of the yeast.

Program to be selected: White bread, level II (750 g), medium browning level.

The bread tastes very good with cheese and also good with jam!

INGREDIENTS

- 50 g Whole meal rye flour type 1150
- 400 g Whole meal flour type 1050
- 1 teaspoon, heaped salt
- 100 g Rye sourdough, recipe from the database
- 260 ml water
- 50 g Seeds or flakes for garnish

PREPARATION

This recipe basically works with all flours, but the rye flour should always be available. All ingredients should be at about the same temperature (room temperature). You can refine it by adding something to the flour: seeds, flakes, onions, bacon or spices. The ideal amount of salt is 1.8 to a maximum of 2 g per 100 g of flour. If you forget the salt, you won't forget it for a lifetime.

First mix 400 g of the desired type of flour with the 50 g whole meal rye flour and the salt. Depending on availability, different flours can also be weighed together in the desired amount. (e.g. 50 g wholegrain rye flour, 200 g wholegrain spelled flour, 200 g

Wholegrain wheat flour) Then I always add the water to the sourdough that has been pulled out and stir it together vigorously. I then add the resulting liquid to the flour mixture.

Knead the mass very well by pulling it apart and whipping it in (for about 30 minutes). Or knead in the food processor with the dough hook at a speed that is not too high (level 2 of 7 levels) until the dough has absorbed all of the flour. Then take the dough out of the container and knead a few times by pressing it flat and then hammering the corners towards the center. You realize that it suddenly becomes more and more difficult. (Do not turn the dough over). Dust some flour on top and place in a bowl with this side down, cover with a cloth and let rest for a few hours.

After about 4 hours, remove the dough, flatten it 3 - 4 times and fold it in again (like last time). Cover and let stand for another 30 minutes.

Then divide the dough into the desired loaves. Press the individual amounts of dough flat again and roll up, cover and let rest for another 30 minutes.

Then flatten the individual portions again and roll them up "across" to the last direction and then finish shaping the loaves into baguettes, rolls, mini loaves, as you like. If you like, press the top briefly into the baking seed, and lay out the whole thing on the baking sheet (on baking paper or similar), cover and let rest for another 30 minutes. Here you will find that the loaves have become really elastic

In the meantime, preheat the oven to approx. 220 ° C (oven room temperature).

Brush the loaves with water or spray, cut into them, (baguettes along the entire length sideways) and immediately put in the oven, middle rack, top and bottom heat, and bake for 20 minutes. (Circulating air is also possible, but choose a lower temperature. Don't be squeamish with the water, bakers even bake with steam)

After 15-20 minutes, brush or spray the loaves again with water. Turn the temperature down by 20 ° C and bake for another 10 minutes. If you "knock" on the underside, it sounds hollow and the crust crackles when you press and release it.

Then take it out and let it cool down a bit.

A tip for leftovers: freeze the whole loaf. Later put frozen in the preheated oven and bake up.

BERLIN BREAD

Servings:1

INGREDIENTS

- 500 g Flour
- 500 g sugar
- 250 g butter
- 2 Egg (s)
- 2 pck. Vanilla sugar
- 1 pck. Baking powder
- 70 g Cocoa powder
- 200 g Hazelnuts, roughly chopped
- 2 tbsp milk
- Grease for the tin

PREPARATION

Mix the butter with the sugar and the eggs then add the remaining ingredients and mix everything well. Spread the dough on a greased baking sheet and secure the front edge from leaking with a folded strip of aluminum foil.

Bake for about 25 minutes at 170 ° C. Carefully cut the bread into square pieces (approx. 1.5 x 1.5 cm) on the tray while it is still warm but no longer hot.

BOILED HAM IN BREAD

Servings:1

INGREDIENTS

- 600 g Boiled ham (pork boiled ham), whole or smoked pork
- For the yeast dough:
- 250 g Rye flour
- 250 g wheat flour
- 1 pck. Dry yeast
- 1 tbsp Turnip tops
- 2 tbsp olive oil
- 1 teaspoon salt
- 375 ml Water, lukewarm
- Possibly. Dry sourdough, about 1 - 2 tbsp

Also:

- Caraway seed
- 1 teaspoon Soda (Imperial Soda)
- 50 ml water

PREPARATION

Knead flour, yeast, turnip greens, oil, salt, water and possibly 1 - 2 tablespoons of dry sourdough with a hand mixer with dough hook in a large bowl for about 5 minutes until the dough comes off the edge.

Briefly preheat the oven to 50 degrees and switch it off. Let the dough rise in the bowl covered with a warm, wet kitchen towel in the switched off oven for 30 minutes.

Knead the dough with a little flour and press it into a round rag. Place the meat in the middle and shape the dough all around into a round bread. Place the dough top down on a baking sheet lined with baking paper or in a round, cast-iron saucepan and leave to rise in the lukewarm, switched-off oven for a maximum of 45 minutes. Make a hole in the bread so that water vapor can escape when baking.

Optionally, in the meantime, boil 50 ml of water with 1 teaspoon of Kaisernatron and let cool down a little. Before baking, brush the baked bread with some of the baking soda solution and sprinkle with caraway seeds.

Briefly take the baked bread out of the oven and preheat the oven to 200 degrees. Place a shallow bowl of hot water on the bottom of the oven. Put the bread on the baking sheet and bake for 55 - 60 minutes. If you knock on it, the bread should sound hollow.

The bread can be eaten warm or cold. To serve, cut the bread with the meat into slices or cut off a cap from the bread, remove the meat, cut into thin slices and pour back into the bread. Then everyone can take out slices with a fork and break off a piece of bread.

BAKING POWDER 4 GRAIN BREAD III

Servings:1

INGREDIENTS

- 150 g   Oats, frozen, ground
- 150 g   Spelled - whole grain, ground
- 150 g   Barley (naked barley), ground
- 50 g   Amaranth, ground
- 1 pinch (s)   Cane sugar
- 1 teaspoon salt
- 1 bag / n   Baking powder (tartar)
- 2 Tea spoons Spice mix for bread OR
- Caraway, coriander, anise + fennel whole or mixed
- 400 ml Sparkling mineral water

PREPARATION

Freeze oats at least 1 hour before grinding. Let all dry ingredients mix together.

Add about 400 ml of carbonated mineral water, on a low level, is enough, let stir well, 5-8 minutes, this also creates a nice crumb.

Pour approx. 750 ml of water into a drip pan under the baking molds.

Place the dough in a small baking pan lined with baking paper or shape into a small loaf, notch the dough + bake.

Since it is not worth using the oven for this small bread, I bake three loaves of bread at the same time. Bake in the cold oven at 160 ° C for approx. 60-70 minutes.

Needle sample.

CORN BREAD DASH

Servings:1

INGREDIENTS

- 500 g Corn kernels, (no popcorn)
- 200 g Chickpeas
- 1 teaspoon Spice mix, (bread spice)
- 1 teaspoon salt
- 1 pinch (s) Cane sugar
- 1 ½ bag / n baking powder
- 400 g Sparkling mineral water
- 500 ml Kefir made from 1.5% milk

PREPARATION

Grind the corn + chickpeas together. Mix all dry ingredients well, add the kefir + water together + stir, it should be like a batter, better a little more liquid, it rises better. Pour the dough into the baking pan lined with baking paper, smooth out + cover with the excess baking paper. Bake in the cold oven at 160 ° C for 70 minutes, nothing more is useful, just the crust will be hard.

Preheat with top + bottom heat to approx. 190 ° C and bake for approx. 45-60 minutes.

With air circulation in the drip pan, which is right at the bottom, pour approx. 500 ml of water, with top + bottom heat put a cup with hot water next to the baking pan.

BREAD ST, ZEZKAZGAN

Servings:1

INGREDIENTS

- 230 g   Dough (sourdough)
- For the dough: (pre-dough)
- 200 g   Corn, ground
- 300 ml Mineral water
- For the dough: (main dough)
- 100 g   Millet, ground
- 50 g   Amaranth, ground
- 50 g   Brown rice, medium grain, ground
- 1 teaspoon Coriander, with grind +
- 1 teaspoon Caraway seeds, with grind
- 1 teaspoon   salt
- 1 pinch (s) Cane sugar
- 125 ml Milk, approx.

PREPARATION

Add the ingredients from the pre-dough to the sourdough + stir, cover with a damp cloth + rest or let rise, at room temperature. Duration one to four hours.

Stir the pre-dough + add all ingredients up to the sugar + let stir, careful with the amount of liquid, possibly more or less, should be viscous.

Pour into a 24 cm loaf pan lined with baking paper, smooth it out and let it rise again at room temperature until the dough has clearly lifted.

Brush the proofed dough with liquid + if the oven is already preheated, bake for approx. 50-60 min at approx. 150 ° C fan oven, otherwise bake in the cold oven at approx. 150 ° C fan oven for approx. 70 min. Needle sample,

Leave in the mold for approx. 10 minutes, carefully take hold of the baking paper + place on the cake rack + unpack + brush with oil or water, cool down + cut with a saw knife from below..

MARES - BREAD

Servings:4

INGREDIENTS

- 1 kg Flour (wheat flour)
- 2 handfuls sugar
- 1 pinch (s) salt
- 1 can Condensed milk
- 1 cube yeast
- water

PREPARATION

Add flour, sugar, and salt to the bowl. Pour condensed milk into a
measuring vessel and fill up to half a liter with warm water.
Important: The liquid must never be too hot. Keep your fingers
clean, ideally you shouldn't feel the liquid at all. The yeast is
crumbled into this liquid (by the way, dry yeast does too).

Stir and knead the dough until it is completely smooth, soft and dry. In the greased form, then let rise in the oven for one hour at 100 degrees, bake for another hour at 200 degrees. Attention, electric stoves are sometimes different. I always put a piece of baking paper on top so that the bread doesn't get too dark on top.

BAKING POWDER - BREAD

Servings:1

INGREDIENTS

- 100 g   Oats, frozen, ground
- 200 g   Spelled - whole grain, ground
- 100 g   Green spelled, ground
- 100 g   Rye - whole grain, ground
- 1 pinch (s) Cane sugar
- 1 teaspoon salt
- 1 bag / n Baking powder (tartar)
- 1 teaspoon Spice mix for bread OR
- Caraway seeds, coriander, anise + fennel whole or ground
- 450 ml Sparkling mineral water

PREPARATION

Freeze oats at least 1 hour before grinding. Mix all dry ingredients.

Add about 450 ml of carbonated mineral water, on a low level, enough, let stir well, 5-8 minutes, this also creates a nice crumb.

Pour approx. 750 ml of water into a drip pan.

Put the dough in a small baking pan lined with baking paper or shape it into a small loaf, notch the dough + bake.

Since it is not worth using the oven for this little bread, I bake three loaves of bread at the same time. After baking, brush the bread with hot water.

Bake in the cold oven at 160 ° C for about 60-70 minutes. Needle sample.

BERLIN BREAD

Servings:1

INGREDIENTS

- 250g butter
- 2 Tea spoons cinnamon
- 1 teaspoon Clove (s), ground
- 300 g Nuts, ground
- 100 g Nuts, whole
- 200 g Almond (half ground + half whole)
- 60 g Cocoa powder
- 2 Egg (s)
- 500 g Flour
- ½ pck. Baking powder
- 1 pinch (s)   salt
- 500 g Sugar (brown farin sugar)

PREPARATION

Mix everything together, then leave in the oven at 150-175 ° C top
and bottom heat for about 35-40 minutes.

It is best cut with an electric knife while it is still warm.

MILK ROLL

Servings:22

INGREDIENTS

For the dough: (pre-dough

- 500 g   Wheat flour 405
- 1 cube Yeast, fresh
- 500 ml Milk, 1.5%
- For the dough:
- 500 g   Wheat flour 405
- 150 g   sugar
- 50 g   Margarine, or butter
- 16 g   salt
- 10 g   Baking malt

For painting:

- Something Milk, 1.5%

PREPARATION

I took this recipe from baker S., the "blogging" baker, and converted it to a normal household amount! The original recipe is designed for 10kg flour and of course with margarine (otherwise it's not GDR rolls) !! The baking malt is optional, but for me it is simply part of it: a matter of taste! The recipe is just super delicious and absolutely sure to succeed! For me, THE recipe at all.

Dissolve the yeast in milk, add to the flour, prepare a pre-dough. Let rise in a warm place until it has doubled (it often says 1 hour for me, doesn't mind!). Then add the remaining ingredients to the pre-dough and mix with the dough hook of the food processor until a homogeneous mass has formed. Another 30 minutes of dough rest (here, too, it has often happened to me that I have left it standing for longer).

Knead the dough again on a lightly floured work surface, this time by hand, and shape into rolls (approx. 80g each). Place on a baking tray lined with baking paper. Brush with milk.

Now preheat the oven. Depending on the device between 200-220 ° C, remember, the oven lamp likes to lie, if possible check the temperature with an oven thermometer, the actual temperature should be around 200 ° C.

Brush the rolls with milk again while they cook. Make a cut just before baking and brush again with milk. Bake in the oven for about 15 minutes, but be careful: they brown quickly because of the lactose! Observe! For the last 5 minutes of the baking time, it is better to push the baking tray in one level lower (with top / bottom heat!).

POTATO PICKS ACCORDING TO GRANDMA'S RECIPE

INGREDIENTS

1 ½ kg Potato

1 cube yeast

1 kg   Flour

1 handful   salt

PREPARATION

Grate the potatoes, sprinkle with the salt. Add half of the flour, crumble the yeast on top. Add the other half of the flour to Ann and mix everything together.

Let the dough rise in an ovenproof container (cover with a kitchen towel) for approx. 1.5 hours at approx. 50 ° C. Then fill a large loaf pan (bread pan) and bake for approx. 1.5 hours at 175 ° C (top / bottom heat).

The result is a large bread. After it has cooled down, it is cut into slices and fried in the pan. You can coat the Pickert with your choice of butter, salted butter, jam or turnip greens. Some even like it with liver sausage.

WHOLEMEAL SPELLED BREAD WITH POPPY SEEDS AND GRAINS

- 500 g   Spelled flour, whole grain
- 100 g Sunflower seeds
- 50 g Poppy seeds, ground
- 20 g linseed
- 50 g Cereal flakes (5-grain flakes)
- 1 tbsp   salt
- 400 ml lukewarm water
- 42 g   Yeast (1 cube)

PREPARATION

Mix the spelled flour with the salt, yeast and grains. The amount of grains can be varied as you like, you can also add pumpkin seeds or other grains if necessary. A smooth dough is prepared with the lukewarm water, which is placed in a warm place to rest for 30 minutes.

Then knead the dough well again and then shape it into a loaf of bread. Personally, I like to bake it in a loaf pan, because it doesn't dry out as much while baking and it's easier to cut later.

The loaf of bread is now cooked in pieces and left to rise at approx. 35 ° C for 30 minutes in the oven. Then you bake the loaf of bread at approx. 200 ° C for another 50 minutes and a super delicious bread is ready.

PARMESAN OREGANO ROLLS

Servings:1

INGREDIENTS

- 250 g   Flour, 405
- 100 g   Spelled flour
- 50 g semolina
- 42 g Yeast, fresh
- 2 Tea spoons   salt
- 1 teaspoon sugar
- 240 ml Water, lukewarm
- 2 tbsp   Parmesan, for sprinkling
- 2 Tea spoons Oregano, dried, for sprinkling

PREPARATION

Add yeast to warm water and dissolve. Put all ingredients in a
bowl and mix, add the yeast water and knead well for 10 minutes.

Let the bowl rise for 20 minutes in a warm place, e.g. in a slightly heated oven.

Preheat the oven to 180 degrees.

Knead the dough lightly, form 12 rolls, place on a baking sheet and let rise for another 10 minutes.

Grate the parmesan and mix with oregano. Brush the rolls with water and cut into them and then sprinkle with the Parmesan oregano mixture and bake for about 25 minutes.

SPELLED BREAD (TM RECIPE)

INGREDIENTS

- 600 g   Whole meal spelled flour
- 500 ml Water, lukewarm
- 250 g   Quark
- 50 g oatmeal
- 1 teaspoon sugar
- 2 Tea spoons   salt
- ½ cube   yeast

PREPARATION

The recipe is for the TM, I made it with the Krups Prep & Cook.
But it should also work with other machines or by hand.

Preheat the oven to 200 ° upper and lower heat. Put a cup of water
in the oven.

Insert kneading and flour knives, fill all ingredients into the pot and start the dough program **P2**

Grease a loaf pan and pour in the batter. Sprinkle with pumpkin seeds or something similar.

After about 10 minutes of baking, cut into the top of the bread. Bake for another 50 minutes. The bread is ready when it sounds hollow.

The bread has a nice crust and stays juicy and fresh for a long time. Have fun trying

CONCLUSION

The bread diet is generally considered suitable for everyday use. Because there are no major changes to be made. However, the 5 meals a day must be adhered to so that fat burning can be set in motion. Therefore, the prognosis for stamina is also quite good. The bread diet can be carried out for several weeks without hesitation. The need to count calories requires careful meal planning. However, the bread diet is not one-sided - if only by the fact that the lunch meal is eaten normally. The bread diet is only for users who can take their time for breakfast and other meals. Because the food should be chewed well.

What is allowed, what is forbidden

It is not permitted to smear thick butter on bread during the bread diet. But it is better to do without butter or margarine entirely. The topping shouldn't be too thick either. One slice of sausage or cheese per bread must be enough. You should drink 2 to 3 liters during the bread diet, namely water, tea or sugar-free fruit juices.

SPORT - NECESSARY?

Exercise or regular sport is not the focus of a bread diet. But it is not harmful to do the sport as before

Similar diets

As in the cabbage diet, the cabbage or in the juice diet different juices, the bread diet focuses on the food bread.

COST OF DIET

Additional costs than those spent on normal grocery shopping do not have to be expected with the bread diet. Whole wheat bread costs a little more than white flour bread. But the differences are not that big. There is also no need to buy organic goods separately. Just like with the other purchases, you only have to pay attention to the freshness of the goods.

WHAT IS ALLOWED, WHAT IS FORBIDDEN

It is not permitted to smear thick butter on bread during the bread diet. But it is better to do without butter or margarine entirely. The topping shouldn't be too thick either. One slice of sausage or cheese per bread must be enough. You should drink 2 to 3 liters during the bread diet, namely water, tea or sugar-free fruit juices.

The recommended duration of the bread diet is four weeks. But it is also possible to extend it. You should lose around two pounds per week.

The daily rations consist of five meals. These must also be adhered to in order to avoid feelings of hunger.

In addition, the organism can use the valuable nutrients optimally in this way. It is also important to drink a lot.

Through the balanced food supply bread diet can, with appropriate calorie close, even for the whole family to be performed. At the same time, it also has the advantage that working people can also use it easily; most meals can be prepared and then taken away.

If done consistently, a weight loss of 2-3 pounds a week can be achieved. Ultimately, the bread diet aims at a change in diet towards fruits and vegetables and healthy carbohydrates and away from meat and fat. The high amount of fiber leads to a long-lasting feeling of satiety.

Healthy Smoothies Cookbook

50 DELICIOUS RECIPES TO LOWER YOUR BLOOD SUGAR LEVEL

Ted Davis

All rights reserved.

Disclaimer

Introduction

A smoothie recipe is a drink made from pureed raw fruit and/or vegetables, using a blender. A smoothie often has a liquid base such as water, fruit juice, dairy products, such as milk, yogurt, ice cream or cottage cheese.

1.Green Smoothie

INGREDIENTS

- ❖ 1 medium frozen avocado

- ❖ 1 cup packed spinach

- ❖ 1 cup sliced frozen banana

- ❖ 1 tablespoon ground flax

- ❖ 1/4 cup frozen cauliflower florets

- ❖ 3 pitted Medjool dates

- ❖ 1.25 cups unsweetened almond milk (or more, to taste)

INSTRUCTIONS

1. Place all ingredients for your green smoothie into a high-speed blender or Vitamix and blend until smooth.

2.Best Strawberry Smoothie

INGREDIENTS

- ❖ cups whole frozen strawberries
- ❖ 1/2 medium banana
- ❖ 1/2 cup plain nonfat Greek yogurt
- ❖ 1 cup 100% orange juice

INSTRUCTIONS

1. Place all ingredients into a high-speed blender and mix on high until smooth.

2. Option to add a little bit more orange juice depending on how thick/thin you like your smoothies.

3. Serve immediately.

3.Peanut Butter Banana Smoothie

INGREDIENTS

- ❖ 2 cups frozen sliced bananas
- ❖ 1/2 cup nonfat Greek yogurt
- ❖ 1/2 tablespoon ground flax seeds
- ❖ 1 cup unsweetened almond milk
- ❖ 1 teaspoon vanilla extract
- ❖ 2 tablespoons all-natural peanut butter

INSTRUCTIONS

1. Place all ingredients into a high-speed blender.
2. Blend on high until smooth. Add more almond milk as needed.
3. Serve immediately.

4.Strawberry Banana Spinach Smoothie

INGREDIENTS

For the Meal Prep Smoothies Bags

- ❖ 2 cups frozen sliced bananas
- ❖ 2 cups frozen whole strawberries
- ❖ 4 cups fresh spinach
- ❖ 4 teaspoons chia seeds

For Serving (for 1 serving)

- ❖ 2 tablespoons vanilla protein powder (any kind)
- ❖ 1/2 cup unsweetened almond milk

INSTRUCTIONS

For the Bag

1. First, line a baking sheet with parchment paper. Then, evenly spread out 2 cups of sliced bananas, 2 cups of whole strawberries. Place in the freezer for about 2 hours or until completely frozen.

2. Next, take 4 quart-size freezer bags and write the date and Strawberry Banana Green Smoothie on the front. Add 1 cup of the frozen fruit, a handful of spinach, and a teaspoon of chia seeds to each bag.

3. Before sealing, make sure you squeeze as much air out as possible to prevent freezer burn. Seal and place in the freezer for later use.

For Blending (for 1 serving)

4. Once you're ready to blend, empty contents of spinach smoothie bag into a high-speed blender.

5. Then, add about 1/2 cup of almond milk and 2 tablespoons of your favorite protein powder.

6. Blend on high for about 1 minute or until everything is blended.

5.Triple Berry Smoothie

INGREDIENTS

- ❖ cups frozen triple berry mix

- ❖ 1 medium frozen banana

- ❖ 1/2 tablespoon chia seeds

- ❖ 1/4 cup vanilla protein powder

- ❖ 1.25 cups unsweetened almond milk

INSTRUCTIONS

2. Place all ingredients in a high-speed blender and mix until smooth.

6.Healthy Banana Protein Shake

INGREDIENTS

- ❖ ¾ cup nonfat Greek yogurt, frozen into cubes

- ❖ 2 cups frozen sliced bananas

- ❖ 1 teaspoon vanilla extract

- ❖ ¼ cup vanilla protein powder (we used Garden of Life Raw Organic Protein)

- ❖ 2 cups milk, any kind (we used Almond Breeze Unsweetened Vanilla Almond Milk)

INSTRUCTIONS

1. First, freeze ¾ cup nonfat Greek Yogurt in an ice cube tray.

2. Once the Greek yogurt has fully frozen, place all ingredients for healthy banana shake into a high-speed blender.

3. Blend until smooth and serve with your favorite toppings.

7.Strawberry Banana Smoothie with Peanut Butter

INGREDIENTS

- ❖ 1 cup frozen strawberries
- ❖ 1 cup frozen sliced banana
- ❖ 1/4 cup nonfat plain Greek yogurt
- ❖ 2 tablespoons all-natural creamy peanut butter
- ❖ 1 tablespoon ground flax seeds
- ❖ 1 teaspoon vanilla extract
- ❖ 1 cup unsweetened almond milk

INSTRUCTIONS

1. Place all ingredients in a high-speed blender and mix until smooth.
2. Serve with a drizzle of peanut butter and fresh fruit.

8.Pumpkin Berry Smoothie

INGREDIENTS

- ❖ 2 tablespoons pumpkin puree
- ❖ 1 tablespoon cashew butter
- ❖ 1 cup frozen blueberries
- ❖ 1/2 frozen banana
- ❖ 1/2 tablespoon flax seed meal
- ❖ 1/2 teaspoon pumpkin pie spice
- ❖ 1 cup almond milk, unsweetened

INSTRUCTIONS

1. Place all ingredients in a high-speed blender and blend on high until smooth.

2. Scrape the sides of the blender and add additional almond milk (1 teaspoon at a time) if smoothie is too thick. Blend until smooth.

3. Serve with homemade granola or fruit toppings and enjoy!

9.The Best Chocolate Protein Shake

INGREDIENTS

- ❖ 1 cup frozen blueberries
- ❖ 1 medium frozen banana
- ❖ 1/4 cup chocolate protein powder (any kind!)
- ❖ 1 tablespoon cocoa powder
- ❖ 1/4 cup nonfat Greek yogurt
- ❖ 2 tablespoons cashew butter
- ❖ 1/2 tablespoon ground flaxseed
- ❖ 1 cup unsweetened plain almond milk

INSTRUCTIONS

1. Place all ingredients into a high-speed blender.

2. Blend on high for around 1 minute, stopping to scrape the sides. You may need to add more milk to thin as needed.

3. Serve immediately!

10.The Best Pumpkin Smoothie

INGREDIENTS

- ❖ 2 medium frozen bananas

- ❖ 1/2 cup unsweetened pumpkin puree

- ❖ 3/4 cup coffee, cold (I just used leftover from the morning's pot!)

- ❖ 3/4 cup milk, any kind

- ❖ 1/2 teaspoon pumpkin pie spice

- ❖ 1 teaspoon maple syrup

INSTRUCTIONS

1. Place all ingredients into a high-speed blender.

2. Blend on high for around 1 minute, stopping to scrape the sides if needed.

3. Serve immediately with your favorite whipped topping.

11.Strawberry BANANA Protein Shake

INGREDIENTS

- ❖ 1.5 cups whole frozen strawberries
- ❖ 1/2 cup frozen sliced banana
- ❖ 1/4 cup vanilla protein powder (any kind will work)
- ❖ 1/3 cup nonfat Greek yogurt
- ❖ 1 cup unsweetened almond milk
- ❖ Optional topping: crushed graham crackers

INSTRUCTIONS

1. Place all ingredients into a high-speed blender and blend until smooth. Add more almond milk as needed depending on preference.

12.Blueberry Banana Smoothie

INGREDIENTS

- ❖ 1 cup frozen blueberries
- ❖ 1 cup frozen sliced bananas
- ❖ 1 tablespoon flax meal
- ❖ 1 cup unsweetened almond milk
- ❖ 1 teaspoon vanilla extract

INSTRUCTIONS

1. Place all ingredients into a high-speed blender and blend until smooth.

13.Starbucks Mocha Frappuccino

Ingredients

- ❖ 1 cup strong black coffee chilled

- ❖ 1/2 medium banana cut into chunks and frozen

- ❖ 2 tablespoons unsweetened cocoa powder

- ❖ 2 tablespoons Bob's Red Mill Chia Seeds

- ❖ 1 tablespoon light agave plus additional to taste

- ❖ 2 teaspoons pure vanilla extract

- ❖ Ice

- ❖ Optional for serving: whipped cream whipped coconut cream, chocolate shavings, chocolate syrup or mini chocolate chips

Instructions

1. Combine the coffee, banana, cocoa powder, chia seeds, agave, and vanilla extract in the bottom of a blender.

2. Blend until smooth, about 30 or so seconds depending upon your blender, then add a small handful of ice cubes, blending until the mixture becomes thick. Continue adding ice cubes until you reach your desired consistency (I like mine fairly thick). Pour into a glass. Garnish as desired and enjoy immediately.

14.Peanut Butter Green Smoothie

INGREDIENTS

- ❖ 2 cups sliced frozen bananas

- ❖ 3 tablespoon all-natural peanut butter

- ❖ 2 tablespoons salted peanuts

- ❖ cups unsweetened almond milk

- ❖ 1 cup spinach, packed

INSTRUCTIONS

2. Place all ingredients for your smoothie into a high-speed blender.

3. Blend on high for 1-2 minutes or until smooth. Option to add more almond milk to thin things out as needed.

4. Top with your favorite topping such as peanut butter and roasted peanuts.

15.Banana Matcha Smoothie

INGREDIENTS

- ❖ 1 cup banana slices, frozen

- ❖ 1 teaspoon matcha powder (we use THIS ONE from Matcha Reserve)

- ❖ 1 cup fresh spinach, packed

- ❖ 2 teaspoons flax seed

- ❖ 1 teaspoon vanilla extract

- ❖ 3/4 cup unsweetened almond milk (or more if needed)

INSTRUCTIONS

1. Place all ingredients in a blender and blend until smooth.

16.Dark Chocolate Date Protein Smoothie

INGREDIENTS

- ❖ 2 frozen bananas, medium
- ❖ 3 medjool dates, pitted
- ❖ 1 cup kale, deboned and chopped
- ❖ 3 tablespoons dark cocoa powder
- ❖ 1/2 teaspoon vanilla extract
- ❖ 1 cup nut milk of your choice

INSTRUCTIONS

1. Place all ingredients into a high-speed blender and mix until smooth.

17.Creamy Strawberry Chia Seed Smoothie

INGREDIENTS

- ❖ 1 cup frozen strawberries

- ❖ 1 medium banana

- ❖ 1/2 cup plain nonfat Greek yogurt

- ❖ 1 cup almond milk, unsweetened

- ❖ 1/2 teaspoon vanilla extract

- ❖ 1 tablespoon chia seeds

INSTRUCTIONS

1. Place all ingredients in a blender or Magic Bullet and blend until smooth! Let sit for a few minutes so that the chia seeds can do their magic (expand and get slimy). Enjoy!

18.Banana Smoothie

INGREDIENTS

- ❖ 2 cups frozen sliced bananas
- ❖ 1/2 cup nonfat plain Greek yogurt
- ❖ 1/2 tablespoon ground flax seeds
- ❖ 1 cup unsweetened plain almond milk
- ❖ 1 teaspoon vanilla extract

INSTRUCTIONS

1. Place all ingredients in a high-speed blender and blend on high until smooth. Option to add more almond milk as needed.

19.Pomegranate Green Smoothie Bowl + Upcoming Travels

INGREDIENTS

- ❖ 1/2 cup frozen strawberries
- ❖ 1 frozen banana, medium
- ❖ 1 cup fresh kale, packed
- ❖ 1/2 cup Greek yogurt
- ❖ 1/2 cup pomegranate juice
- ❖ 1/2 cup water
- ❖ 1 scoop vanilla protein powder (any kind!)
- ❖ toppings: hemp seeds, pomegranate arils, pistachio nuts, and dark chocolate

INSTRUCTIONS

1. Place all ingredients in a high-speed food processor and mix until smooth. You may need to add a bit more pomegranate juice depending on how thick you like your smoothies.

20.Apple Pie Smoothie Bowl

INGREDIENTS

- ❖ 1 frozen banana, small

- ❖ 1/2 cup non-fat vanilla Greek yogurt*

- ❖ 2/3 cup apple sauce, unsweetened

- ❖ 1/4 cup rolled oats**

- ❖ 1 teaspoon cinnamon

- ❖ 1 teaspoon vanilla extract

- ❖ 1/2 cup almond milk, unsweetened

- ❖ optional: handful of fresh spinach or kale

INSTRUCTIONS

1. Place all ingredients in a high-speed blender. Blend until smooth.

2. Serve with lots of fixings on top!

21.Blueberry Spinach Smoothie

INGREDIENTS

- ❖ 1 large banana
- ❖ 1 cup nonfat Greek yogurt
- ❖ 1 cup fresh blueberries
- ❖ 2 cups packed spinach
- ❖ 1 cup 100% orange juice
- ❖ 1 teaspoon fresh ginger, peeled and grated
- ❖ 2–3 cups of ice

INSTRUCTIONS

1. Place all ingredients in a high-speed blender and mix until smooth.

22.Peanut Butter and Jelly Protein Smoothie

INGREDIENTS

- ❖ 1 cup mixed frozen berries

- ❖ 1–2 tablespoons all-natural peanut butter

- ❖ 1/4 cup vanilla protein powder (we love Organic Valley) *

- ❖ 2 tablespoons rolled oats

- ❖ 1 cup milk, any kind

INSTRUCTIONS

1. Place all ingredients in a blender and mix until smooth.

23.Apple Smoothie

INGREDIENTS

- ❖ 2 4-oz. apple sauce cups, frozen*

- ❖ 1 cup unsweetened almond milk (or any kind of milk)

- ❖ 2 tablespoons rolled oats

- ❖ 2 tablespoons nut butter (any kind)

- ❖ 1 teaspoon ground flax seed

- ❖ 1 teaspoon maple syrup

- ❖ 1/4 teaspoon ground cinnamon

INSTRUCTIONS

1. First, freeze 2 4-oz. applesauce cups for at least 2 hours or overnight.

2. Once frozen, run the applesauce cups under hot water for a few seconds to remove from the plastic. Then place into a high-speed blender.

3. Add the rest of the ingredients and cover.

4. Blend on high for around a minute or until smooth.

24.Strawberry Pineapple Smoothie

INGREDIENTS

- ❖ cups frozen pineapple chunks

- ❖ cups frozen strawberries

- ❖ 1/2 cup vanilla Greek yogurt

- ❖ 1 teaspoon vanilla extract

- ❖ cups almond milk, unsweetened (or more to taste)

INSTRUCTIONS

1. Place all ingredients for your strawberry pineapple smoothie into a high-speed blender.

2. Blend on high until smooth. Depending on how frozen your fruit is, you may need to add more almond milk.

3. Serve with extra fresh pineapple chunks on the bottom.

25.Magical Orange Creamsicle Smoothie

INGREDIENTS

1. 1 cup frozen banana slices

2. 1 teaspoon vanilla extract

3. 1 cup 100% orange juice

4. optional: 1/2 cup ice

5. optional: 1 scoop vanilla protein powder, coconut whipped cream, orange zest

INSTRUCTIONS

1. Place frozen bananas, vanilla extract, and orange juice into a high-speed blender and blend until smooth.

2. Option at this point to add a handful of ice (depending on thickness preference) and/or other add-ins such as vanilla protein powder and fresh orange zest.

3. Blend one more time and then serve immediately.

26.Healthy Chocolate Peanut Butter Smoothie

INGREDIENTS

- ❖ 2 cups sliced frozen bananas

- ❖ 3 tablespoons all-natural creamy peanut butter

- ❖ 1/4 cup cocoa powder

- ❖ 1 tablespoon ground flaxseed

- ❖ 1 cup packed spinach

- ❖ 1 cup almond milk

INSTRUCTIONS

1. Remove frozen bananas from the freezer and place them into a high-speed blender.

2. Next, add the rest of the ingredients to the blender and blend until smooth.

3. If the smoothie is too thick, slowly add a tablespoon of almond milk at a time until smoothie reaches desired consistency.

27.Blueberry Date Smoothie Bowls

INGREDIENTS

- ❖ 1 banana, frozen
- ❖ 1 cup blueberries, frozen
- ❖ 2 medjool dates
- ❖ 1 tablespoon chia seeds
- ❖ 1 cup almond milk, unsweetened
- ❖ optional: 1 scoop vanilla protein powder
- ❖ Toppings: medjool dates, kiwi, blueberries, flaked coconut, and chia seeds

INSTRUCTIONS

1. Place all ingredients into a high-speed blender and blend until smooth. Top with chopped medjool dates, kiwi, blueberries, flaked coconut, and chia seeds.

28.Mango Smoothie

INGREDIENTS

- ❖ 2 cups frozen mango slices
- ❖ 1 15-oz. can light coconut milk
- ❖ 1/2 tablespoon flaxseed meal
- ❖ 1 large frozen banana

INSTRUCTIONS

1. Place all of the ingredients into a high-speed blender.
2. Blend on high until smooth.
3. Eat immediately.

29.Kale Smoothie

INGREDIENTS

- ❖ 2 cups frozen bananas
- ❖ 2 cups packed chopped kale
- ❖ 1 tablespoon flax meal
- ❖ 2 Medjool dates, pitted
- ❖ optional: 1/2 teaspoon fresh grated ginger
- ❖ cups orange juice

INSTRUCTIONS

1. Place all ingredients in a high-speed blender.

2. Blend on high until smooth. Option to add more orange juice as needed to thin things out.

3. Serve smoothie immediately and top with your favorite toppings.

30.Golden Milk Mango Smoothie

ingredients

- ❖ 1 teaspoon turmeric (you could totally leave this out if you want a plain mango smoothie!)

- ❖ Frozen mango 1 cup

- ❖ ¾ cup yogurt any kind

- ❖ 1 frozen banana or 1 cup of cauliflower

- ❖ optional: splash of milk or water if you need help getting the blender going

instructions

1. In a high-speed blender, combine all of the ingredients and blend until smooth. If needed, add more liquid, a tablespoon at a time, to get the blender going. I like my smoothies on the thicker side but add some milk/ water as needed.

2. Serve and ENJOY!

31.Carrot Cake Smoothie

ingredients

- ❖ 8 walnuts

- ❖ 1 large carrot, roughly chopped (or grated if you don't have a high-speed blender)

- ❖ Extra finely grated carrot for mixing in, optional

- ❖ 1 teaspoon of cinnamon

- ❖ Sprinkle of nutmeg, freshly grated is EXTRA delicious

- ❖ 2 pitted dates

- ❖ ½–1 cup of liquid, I typically use non-dairy milk and then add in water if I want it a bit more liquidly

- ❖ 1 teaspoon of vanilla

- ❖ ½ of a frozen banana

instructions

1. In a high-speed blender, blend all ingredients (minus the additional carrot) together until creamy and smooth.

2. If desired, mix in additional finely grated carrot (highly recommend!). Top with a few chopped walnuts and ENJOY!

32.Caramel Apple Green Smoothie

ingredients

- ❖ 1 green apple
- ❖ 2 handfuls of greens
- ❖ pinch of sea salt
- ❖ 1 tablespoon of hemp seeds
- ❖ 1 frozen banana (could leave this out but sub for a few ice cubes)
- ❖ almond milk (could substitute for apple juice for a stronger apple taste)
- ❖ sprinkle of cinnamon (or a couple sprinkles)
- ❖ 2 pitted dates
- ❖ Vegan Caramel Sauce from Pinch of Yum

instructions

1. Add all of the ingredients (minus the caramel) to a high-speed blender and blend on high.

2. Drizzle a little of the caramel sauce around your glass and pour the smoothie into the glass.

3. Top with a bit more of the caramel sauce and ENJOY!

4. Eat a spoonful of the caramel sauce by the spoonful ;)

33.Oatmeal Smoothie

Ingredients

- ❖ 1/4 cup old-fashioned oats or quick oats
- ❖ 1 banana chopped into chunks and frozen
- ❖ 1/2 cup unsweetened almond milk
- ❖ 1 tablespoon creamy peanut butter
- ❖ 1/2 tablespoon pure maple syrup plus additional to taste
- ❖ 1/2 teaspoon pure vanilla extract
- ❖ 1/2 teaspoon ground cinnamon
- ❖ 1/8 teaspoon kosher salt don't skip this, as it makes the oatmeal pop!
- ❖ Ice optional, add at the end if you want a thicker smoothie

Instructions

1. Place the oats in the bottom of a blender and pulse a few times until finely ground. Add the banana, milk, peanut butter, maple syrup, vanilla, cinnamon, and salt.

2. Blend until smooth and creamy, stopping to scrape down the blender as needed. Taste and add additional sweetener if you'd like a sweeter smoothie. Enjoy immediately.

34.Blueberry Date Shake

Ingredients

- ❖ 2 medium bananas cut into chunks and frozen (about 8 ounces or 1 1/2 cups slices)

- ❖ 1 cup frozen blueberries about 4 ounces

- ❖ 3 pitted Medjool dates plus additional to taste

- ❖ 1 tablespoon almond butter plus additional to taste

- ❖ 1/2 teaspoon pure vanilla extract

- ❖ 1 cup Almond Breeze almond milk Unsweetened Vanilla

- ❖ 2-3 ice cubes optional

Instructions

1. Place the banana, blueberries, dates, almond butter, vanilla extract, and almond milk in a high-powered blender (if you do not have a high-powered blender, I recommending blending the milk and half of the frozen fruit first, then slowing adding the rest of the fruit and remaining ingredients).

2. Blend until smooth. If you would like the shake a bit thicker, add a few ice cubes and blend again. Taste and add additional almond butter if you'd like the shake a little richer or another date if you'd like it sweeter. Pour and enjoy

35.Beet Smoothie

Ingredients

- ❖ 1/2 cup unsweetened almond milk or milk of choice

- ❖ 1 cup mixed frozen blueberries or mixed berries

- ❖ 1 small beet peeled and diced (about 8 ounces)

- ❖ 1/4 cup frozen pineapple

- ❖ 1/4 cup plain nonfat Greek yogurt use non-dairy yogurt to make vegan

- ❖ Optional sweetener: 1-2 teaspoons honey plus additional to taste (use agave to make vegan)

- ❖ Optional mix-ins: chia seeds hempseed, and/or ground flaxseed (I like mine with a sprinkle of chia or hempseed; hempseed is what you see pictured in the photos); I also like to add 2 tablespoons oatmeal to make the smoothie even more filling.

Instructions

1. Place the almond milk, blueberries, beet, pineapple, and Greek yogurt in a high-speed blender such as a Vitamix (if you do not have a high-speed blender, I'd suggest microwaving, roasting, or lightly steaming the beets before using so that they are softer and puree more smoothly).

2. Blend until smooth. Taste and if you desire a sweeter smoothie, add a little honey or date and blend again. Enjoy immediately or refrigerate for up to 1 day.

36.Berry Turmeric Smoothie

Ingredients

- ❖ 3/4 cup unsweetened vanilla almond milk or milk of choice

- ❖ 2 cups baby spinach about 2 large handfuls

- ❖ 1/2 cup nonfat plain Greek yogurt or dairy-free yogurt of choice

- ❖ 3 tablespoons old-fashioned rolled oats

- ❖ 1 1/2 cups frozen mixed berries I used a blend of blackberries, blueberries, and raspberries

- ❖ 1/2 teaspoon McCormick Ground Turmeric

- ❖ 1/4 teaspoon McCormick Ground Ginger

- ❖ 2-3 teaspoons honey or swap agave or maple syrup to make vegan, plus additional to taste

Instructions

1. Place the ingredients in a high-powered blender in the order listed: almond milk, spinach, yogurt, oats, berries, turmeric, ginger, and 2 teaspoons honey.

2. Blend until smooth. Taste and adjust sweetness as desired. If you do not have a high-powered blender, I recommend blending the almond milk, spinach, and yogurt first, and then adding the other ingredients. Enjoy immediately.

37.Cleansing Apple Avocado Smoothie

Ingredients

- ❖ 1 cup plain unsweetened almond milk

- ❖ 4 cups loosely packed spinach that's about 2 large handfuls

- ❖ 1 medium avocado peeled and pitted

- ❖ 2 medium apples any kind you like, peel on, cored and quartered (if not using a high-powered blender such as a Vitamix, cut into a rough dice)

- ❖ 1 medium banana cut into chunks and frozen

- ❖ 2 teaspoons honey or maple syrup plus additional to taste

- ❖ 1/2 teaspoon ground ginger or 1/4-inch knob of fresh ginger (if not using a high-power blender, mince the ginger first; use less than 1/2 teaspoon if you'd like a more subtle taste. This smoothie has some zip!)

- ❖ Small handful of ice cubes

- ❖ Optional additions: chia seeds flaxseed, protein powder, almond butter or other nut butter of choice

Instructions

1. In the order listed, add the almond milk, spinach, avocado, apples, banana, honey, ginger, and ice to a high-powered blender.

2. Blend until smooth. Taste and adjust sweetness and spices as desired. Enjoy immediately.

38.Coconut Chocolate Mint Chip Smoothie

INGREDIENTS

- ❖ 1 cup unsweetened almond, cashew or coconut milk
- ❖ 1/2 coconut water (or more milk)
- ❖ 1–2 Tablespoons coconut butter or frozen coconut
- ❖ 1/2–1 cup frozen cauliflower rice
- ❖ 1 scoop chocolate protein powder
- ❖ 1 Tablespoon chia seeds
- ❖ 1/2 Tablespoon cacao or cocoa powder
- ❖ 4–5 fresh mint leaves or 1–2 drops of peppermint extract
- ❖ 1–2 teaspoons cacao nibs
- ❖ granola, for topping (optional)

INSTRUCTIONS

1. Blend all ingredients except cacao nibs and granola in a high-powered blender.

2. Blend until smooth. Add in cacao nibs and blend a couple seconds more. Pour into a glass, sprinkle with granola and cacao nibs and enjoy!

39.Maqui Berry Smoothie Bowl

INGREDIENTS

- ❖ 1 cup unsweetened vanilla almond milk
- ❖ 1 cup frozen cauliflower
- ❖ 1 cup frozen blueberries
- ❖ 1 Tablespoon coconut butter (almond butter works too)
- ❖ 2 scoops vanilla protein powder
- ❖ 2 Tablespoons wild maqui berry powder
- ❖ toppings of choice: goji berries, superfood maca granola, cacao nibs, unsweetened shredded coconut, chia seeds and fresh fruit

INSTRUCTIONS

1. Add ingredients into a high-powered blender in the order listed and blend until smooth and creamy. Add more almond milk if you want the texture to be thinner. Serve in a bowl with your favorite toppings.

40.Chocolate Almond Crispy Bites

INGREDIENTS

- ❖ 2/3 cup almond butter (runny almond butter from a fresh jar works best) *

- ❖ 1/3 cup brown rice syrup

- ❖ 3 cups chocolate brown rice crispy cereal (like Nature's Path Koala Crisp)

- ❖ 1/4 cup almonds, chopped

- ❖ 1/8 cup cacao nibs or mini vegan chocolate chips (optional)

INSTRUCTIONS

1. Pour almond butter and brown rice syrup into a bowl and stir to combine.

2. Add cereal, almonds and cacao nibs/chocolate chips if using. Stir to coat evenly. It may take a few minutes and using your hands can be helpful. If the mixture doesn't seem to be sticking together well you can add additional brown rice syrup (one tablespoon at a time).

3. Place mixing bowl in the fridge to allow the mixture to setup for 5-10 minutes. Using your hands, grab 1-2 Tablespoons worth of the mixture and roll into balls. If you're having trouble, try using wet hands to roll the bites. Place bites on parchment paper. Transfer bites to the fridge until ready to serve. Enjoy!

41.Grapefruit Smoothie

INGREDIENTS

- ❖ 1 Winter Sweets red grapefruit

- ❖ 2 cups frozen pineapple chunks

- ❖ 1/3 cup Greek yogurt

- ❖ 1 Tablespoon coconut oil

- ❖ 1/4-inch knob of fresh ginger

- ❖ grapefruit segments, berries and granola (for topping)

INSTRUCTIONS

1. Segment grapefruit over a bowl so you can collect all the juice. Set 2-3 segments aside for topping. Add grapefruit segments, grapefruit juice, frozen pineapple, Greek yogurt, coconut oil and fresh ginger into a high-powered blender and blend until smooth. Taste and adjust ingredients based on your preference. If smoothie is too thick you can add a little non-dairy milk.

2. Pour into two glasses and enjoy. Or serve in a bowl with your favorite toppings — grapefruit segments, granola, berries, etc.

42.Paleo Purple Sweet Potato Smoothie [with cauliflower!]

INGREDIENTS

- ❖ 1 cup cubed purple sweet potato, pre-cooked & frozen
- ❖ 1 cup frozen cauliflower rice*
- ❖ 1 cup unsweetened coconut milk**
- ❖ 1/2 TBS ginger paste, or 1
- ❖ 1 tsp maca powder
- ❖ 1 large Medjool date***, pitted
- ❖ 1 TBS cashew butter

INSTRUCTIONS

1. Add all ingredients to blender cup.

2. Blend until smooth.

3. Add more (or less) liquid for desired consistency. I used 1 cup of milk and it was fairly thick. Add more liquid or milk to drink through straw.

43.Chai Pumpkin Protein Smoothie [no powder!]

INGREDIENTS

- ❖ 1/3 cup All Whites 100% liquid egg whites

- ❖ 2 Medjool dates, pitted (or sub another sweetener such as 1/2 TBS maple syrup)

- ❖ 1/2 cup pumpkin puree* (option to freeze into cubes)

- ❖ 1/2 TBS cashew butter

- ❖ 1 tsp pumpkin pie spice**

- ❖ 1/2 tsp ground cardamom

- ❖ 2/3 cup*** cashew milk (or milk of choice)

INSTRUCTIONS

1. Place all ingredients into blender cup starting with All Whites 100% liquid egg whites, ending with cashew milk. See notes below regarding frozen pumpkin versus fresh and amount of milk needed.

2. Blend until smooth.

3. Transfer pumpkin protein smoothie into cup or travel mug, enjoy!

44.Creamy Citrus Ginger Smoothie

INGREDIENTS

- ❖ 2 Navel Oranges, peeled and segmented

- ❖ 1/2 cup coconut milk (or milk of choice)

- ❖ 1 1" cube fresh ginger, skin removed and chopped

- ❖ 1 cup ice

INSTRUCTIONS

1. Add all of the ingredients into blender – make sure your oranges are segmented if you prefer a more pulp-free orange juice. 2. Blend until smooth. Add more ice or liquid for desired consistency.

45.Cinnamon Cherry Berry Date Smoothie

INGREDIENTS

- ❖ 3/4 cup frozen tart red cherries (make sure they're pitted!)

- ❖ 1/4 cup frozen blueberries

- ❖ 1/4 cup whole frozen strawberries

- ❖ 2 Medjool Dates, pitted

- ❖ 3/4 cup coconut milk (or liquid of choice, but I suggest something creamy)

- ❖ 1 tsp ground cinnamon

- ❖ ½ tsp ground ginger (or 1" peeled fresh cube)

- ❖ optional add-ins:

- ❖ 1 TBS hemp hearts

- ❖ 2 cups greens

- ❖ 2 servings favorite protein powder* (I like vanilla or unflavored here)

INSTRUCTIONS

1. Add everything to blender, starting with fruit and ending with liquid and protein powder. If using NutriBullet, make sure you follow order of ingredients listed.

2. Blend until smooth. Adjust liquid or add ice to achieve desired consistency.

3. Divide into smoothie into two glasses, enjoy!

46.Purple Power Superfood Smoothie

INGREDIENTS

- ❖ 1/3 cup liquid of choice (coconut water, unsweetened non-dairy milk, water)

- ❖ 1/3 cup frozen cherries

- ❖ 1/3 cup whole frozen strawberries

- ❖ 1/4 cup frozen blueberries

- ❖ 1 tsp acai powder

- ❖ optional add-ins:

- ❖ protein powder

- ❖ nut butter

- ❖ spinach

- ❖ milled flaxseed

- ❖ maca powder

INSTRUCTIONS

1. Add all ingredients into your blender. If using a small blender such as a NutriBullet, add your add-ins last. Blend ingredients together until smooth. Adjust liquid as necessary to desired consistency.

47.ANTIOXIDANT SMOOTHIE FREEZER PACK

INGREDIENTS

- ❖ 1 cup (5 ounces) frozen berries
- ❖ 1 banana, sliced
- ❖ 1/2 cup baby spinach
- ❖ 1 tablespoon flax seeds
- ❖ 1 tablespoon cocoa powder
- ❖ 1 tablespoon maple syrup
- ❖ 1 cup almond milk (more as needed)
- ❖ 1 scoop collagen peptides (optional)

INSTRUCTIONS

To Make Freezer Packs:

2. Place all ingredients, except almond milk, into a freezer safe bag. Freeze until ready to use, up to 1 month.

To blend:

3. Combine all ingredients, including almond milk, in a high-speed blender.

4. Blend until creamy, adding additional almond milk if necessary.

48.COFFEE BANANA SMOOTHIE

INGREDIENTS

- ❖ 1/2 cup unsweetened almond milk or milk of choice

- ❖ 1/2 cup freshly brewed organic coffee or cold brew, place in fridge for 10 minutes

- ❖ 1 frozen banana

- ❖ 1 scoop protein powder (I like Vital Proteins Collagen Peptides)

- ❖ 1/2 tablespoon chia seeds

- ❖ Optional: 1 teaspoon honey or sweetener of choice

- ❖ Optional: Handful of ice cubes

INSTRUCTIONS

1. Combine all ingredients in a high-speed blender.

2. Blend until creamy.

3. Taste and add additional sweetener if needed.

49.SUPERFOOD SUMMER FRUIT SMOOTHIE

INGREDIENTS

- ❖ 1/2 frozen banana
- ❖ 1 Kiwi, skin peeled
- ❖ 1/4 cup frozen pineapple
- ❖ 1/2 cup frozen strawberry
- ❖ 1/4 cup frozen Peaches
- ❖ 1/2 cup frozen Raspberry
- ❖ 1 teaspoon grated ginger, more to taste
- ❖ 1 teaspoon chia seeds
- ❖ 2 cups cashew milk, or nut-milk of choice, add more based on desired consistency
- ❖ 1/4 teaspoon cinnamon, more for garnish
- ❖ Optional: 1/4 cup cauliflower, frozen
- ❖ Optional: 1 teaspoon bee pollen, either blended in or used as a garnish
- ❖ Optional: 1 teaspoon ground flaxseeds
- ❖ Optional: 1 scoop protein powder of choice

INSTRUCTIONS

1. Place all ingredients in a high-speed blender. Blend until smooth. If too thick, add more liquid and blend longer. Serve right away!

50.ANTI-INFLAMMATORY SMOOTHIE FREEZER PACK

INGREDIENTS

- ❖ 1 cup (5 ounces) frozen mango
- ❖ 1/2 cup (2 ounces) frozen cauliflower florets
- ❖ 1 banana, sliced
- ❖ 1" piece of fresh ginger, peeled
- ❖ 1" piece fresh turmeric, peeled
- ❖ pinch fresh black pepper
- ❖ pinch cinnamon
- ❖ 1 cup canned coconut milk
- ❖ 1/2 cup water
- ❖ 1 scoop collagen peptides (optional)

INSTRUCTIONS

To Make Freezer Packs:

2. Place all ingredients except coconut milk and water into a freezer safe bag. Freeze until ready to use, up to 1 month.

To blend:

3. Combine all ingredients, including coconut milk and water in a high-speed blender.

CONCLUSION

Whether you're looking for a way to add some nutrition to your daily diet or seeking to learn more about smoothies to begin your first cleanse, you now have some excellent recipes and tips to get you started. Remember, though, to use this as a general guide. Once you get the hang of mixing flavors, feel free to make up your own blends to suit your tastes and health goals.

Blend until creamy, adding additional water if necessary.

Lightning Source UK Ltd.
Milton Keynes UK
UKHW022208050421
381481UK00007B/123